T0152341

Bad Things, Good People, and God

A Guide for Teens

Bryan Bliss

 Morehouse Publishing
NEW YORK

Morehouse Publishing, 19 East 34th Street, New York, NY 10016

Morehouse Publishing is an imprint of Church Publishing Incorporated.

Cover design by Jennifer Kopec, 2Pug Design
Typeset by PerfecType, Nashville, Tennessee

Library of Congress Cataloging-in-Publication Data

Names: Bliss, Bryan, author.
Title: Bad things, good people, and God : a guide for teens / Bryan Bliss.
Description: New York, NY : Morehouse Publishing, [2022] | Audience: Ages
   13-18 | Audience: Grades 7-9
Identifiers: LCCN 2021041341 (print) | LCCN 2021041342 (ebook) | ISBN
   9781640654822 (paperback) | ISBN 9781640654839 (epub)
Subjects: LCSH: Suffering--Religious aspects--Christianity. | Good and
   evil--Religious aspects--Christianity. | Theodicy. | Christian
   teenagers--Religious life.
Classification: LCC BV4909 .B55 2022 (print) | LCC BV4909 (ebook) | DDC
   248.8/6--dc23
LC record available at https://lccn.loc.gov/2021041341
LC ebook record available at https://lccn.loc.gov/2021041342

Contents

Contents

Introduction

Congratulations!

By picking up this book, you've—perhaps unintentionally—joined a discourse that has been happening . . . well, since people could talk. And complain. So, by "congratulations" of course I mean I'm terribly sorry.

That all said, bad things happen. We know this.

But *why*?

This is a question that has nagged theologians and philosophers—people like you—for centuries. *Millennia,* actually.

Basically forever.

But should it be such a difficult question? If we believe in a God who loves us, shouldn't evil just . . . disappear? Shouldn't it be as simple as saying, "I believe," or, even better, having God say, "I got this," and then—poof!—all of our pain, our hurt, the brokenness of the world, is gone.

Of course, this isn't the case.

And if we're being honest, most of the answers that have been offered for this question aren't exactly . . . comprehensive. It doesn't help that you have to contend with the Bible, centuries of theological hot takes, lived experiences, and, you know, the nagging doubt that none of this is real and we're all just floating through the universe untethered from *anything* . . .

Let's take a deep breath.

Just because there isn't an easy answer (any answer?) to the problem of evil—why bad things happen—doesn't mean we need to live in a state of constant anxiety or dread. It is not an overstatement to say this is *the biggest question of faith*. It's also a question that all of us must wrestle with, cobble together some semblance of an answer, and claim our place as theologians in the world.

Yes, *theologians*.

Because what you have to say *matters*. Your theology *matters*. Your view of the world reveals another glimmer of truth—some small answer—to these big questions.

So, what do you think?

Are you ready to think through one of the biggest questions of faith?

Along the way we'll look at the Bible, give a serious side-eye to some of the "classic" attempts at answering this question, think about sin and suffering, and come out the other side without a single scratch.

(Well, no promises on that last bit. You might be reading this in a hammock, get so excited by your new insights that you rush off to tell somebody, and fall to the ground. But be assured: the book itself will not cause you harm.)

A quick warning: by the end, you're going to have more questions.

It's inevitable.

But the questions will make things a little clearer. Hopefully they'll give you a glimpse of a path forward.

Because we're all doing this one step at a time.

Are you ready?

1

Houston, We Have a Problem

$\int$ ome words are just fun to say.

Like, *juniper*. That's a good one—it feels like a fun word, doesn't it? Oh! What about . . . *barista*? Say that one out loud right now—*barista!* See, you're having fun. You're smiling. You can't help it. The world is your oyster.

Hey, want to know a word that isn't any fun at all and, let's face it, is pretty much the worst word ever invented in the entire history of language?

Theodicy.

Nope. Don't like that one.

Saying *theodicy* is like biting down on tinfoil. It's like somebody is getting ready to hand you a big bowl of popcorn and just as you reach for that buttery, salty goodness, they dump it on the ground intentionally.

Theodicy is a rude word. A harsh word. A confusing word.

No thanks.

But if we're going to talk about suffering—about why bad things happen—we need to also talk about theodicy. As gross a word as it is, it's also the word that is used by theologians to describe the conversation that asks why things like sickness, poverty, death—all of it—exist in the world and how God is involved.

Do you need to know this word? Not really. It's a fancy word, strutting around with its nose in the air. That said, if you happen to be at coffee hour and you see your priest or pastor and you say, "Sometimes I find myself considering *theodicy* and just find myself so . . . vexed," that's what you call a "power move."

Perhaps less importantly, it's also the word that starts our conversation.

Bad things happen. People suffer. This is theodicy.

If we break the word down, we get two Greek words—*Theos* and *dikē*. *Theos* is translated as "God" and *dikē* is often translated as "trial" or "judgment." So, when you put those together, the word "theodicy" is about asking big questions—about "justifying God."

This might seem strange—why would we need to justify God? Isn't the point of, well, being God that you *don't* have to justify God's self? That what you do is what you *do* and people are left to simply deal with the repercussions?

Well, yeah. That's the crux of the problem, isn't it?

Let's do this a different way.

What are some words you would use to describe God?

2

Take a second, but here's a few:

"Loving." "All-knowing." "The Good Shepherd."

You likely came up with some different ones but these, typically, give us a pretty good look at who and what God is. The problem materializes when something bad—either big or small—happens. For some people, it's easy to chalk that up to "God's will" (don't worry, we'll talk about that one later . . .) or the idea that, if God wants something to happen it's going to happen, so buckle up and *learn something* from all this pain and grief. Now, normal people who are not complete psychopaths would hear that argument and think, "Hmm. This doesn't seem to add up. Let's check our math."

A Good and Loving God Who Is Omniscient, Omnipresent, Omnipotent	+	The Mere Existence of Hungry Children	=	Yeah, Only a Complete Psycho Wouldn't Have Any Questions

We, friends, are not complete psychos. And I'm betting you have questions.

These questions—which, again, have troubled humans for the entirety of our existence—are what make up theodicy. They are questions that have some general boundaries, a few similarities, but they are also wildly personal, completely dependent on your experiences.

We all have working theodicies. We all have questions. The trick is knowing how we think—we call that *doing theology*, kids—and whether that conception of God is harming us or those around us.

Because while there aren't many answers in this little book, I can say this without a doubt: God is not in the business of harm.

If God is not in the business of harm and there are still all these bad things happening—seemingly every second of the day—then we must deal with the question of theodicy. Of suffering. Because, let's face it, the world isn't supposed to be this way. And for those of us who risk a life believing and following God, we must contend with the fact that, unlike God, evil provides its own evidence.

This doesn't mean that God isn't real.

And it doesn't mean that we don't experience God in deep and meaningful ways.

But it does mean that, for us to grow in our faith—for it to mature—we need to spend time wrestling with big questions. And like Jacob, who wrestled with God, it's not necessarily something that will leave us unmarked (Genesis 32:22–32). There is a very good chance that, after reading a book like this, you will not be able to "un-see" the problem of theodicy.

It might not seem like it, but that's a good thing, especially as your faith becomes more nuanced. The excitement of a life of faith is tied up in the risk of tackling these sorts of questions. Think of it this way: being a seven-foot-tall professional basketball player competing against high school kids sounds like fun, but at some point, dunking on everybody is going to get boring. The same goes with faith. The longer we're in it, the longer we're connected to this whole Jesus thing, the more we're going to want to see the hoop raised.

> **Jesus Christ**, son of God, fully human. Born in Palestine, sometime around 1 CE, died by execution via the Roman Empire (again, sometime around) 33 CE and then—depending on who and what you believe—rose again three days later and proceeded to become the basis for a faith tradition that has 2.38 billion followers. Kind of a big deal.

But it's not necessary! For many people, this sort of theological growth—the idea of wrestling with God and walking the rest of your life with a jacked-up hip bone—is . . . not a priority. So instead of dealing with the big questions, they develop pat theological responses that don't come close to providing a real answer.

You've likely experienced this already.

Somebody passes away and . . . *God must've needed another angel.*

Somebody gets sick and . . . *God has a plan.*

Something destructive happens and . . . *God is trying to teach you something.*

No, no, and *no.*

No!

Listen, it's completely okay if this sort of answer makes you feel better. There is something calming about believing we're all tied up in a massive divine plan that can't possibly be understood. The little bumps (and the big ones too!) become temporary inconveniences on our path to heaven. Or, as one famous Christian music group once said to a room full of teenagers, "God doesn't know the ends without planning the means."

Speaking of famous Christian music groups and bad theology, a certain author of a certain book may or may not have yelled out "No!" to this stance and was politely asked to leave. Allegedly.

That sort of theology is easy. And it can remain easy for a long, long time. But it ultimately has an expiration date. There's no telling when easy theology—those quick-fix answers—will no longer fit. At some point they won't. And then you will be left to reckon with a God who is willing to allow war and famine, sickness and abuse *now*, because in the afterlife you will find peace. A God who seems to only care about what happens to you in the end, not during the beautiful, messy moments of the life you're living right now.

The question is: What do you want?

Do you want the easy, temporary answer?

Or do you want to risk something? Do you want to tangle with the wild and sometimes unsafe—but always good—God and see what happens? See where you end up. It's okay if this makes you nervous. That's normal. And perhaps the way we should all do theology is to show up, to open ourselves to the possibilities God has in store for us, and say the most dangerous words any Christian can say: "I'm ready, God. Let's do this."

In the Beginning...

Let's start at the beginning.

And by "the beginning" I mean, literally, *"In the beginning . . ."* (Genesis 1:1).

Creationism—or the idea that God made the earth, all of us, everything—is both a beautiful theological concept and one that comes with a host of theological problems and contradictions to modern science. And the way it is sometimes referred to today—as a literal, historical account—is not only a recent construct but also, despite all the press it gets, not something most Christians *believe.*

Let's not start with the negative (which, admittedly, is hard when you're talking about theodicy) but with the beauty of creation.

Have you ever stood on a beach at sunrise?

Have you ever hiked to the top of a mountain and paused just to take in the majesty of it all?

Consider the miracle of our bodies, our abilities to create, think, play, laugh, and love.

Even if you don't believe in a literal seven-day creation, the theology of the Genesis story can be beautiful. It reminds us that God is the bringer of light and the One who turns chaos into order and, so many times, that order leads to shocking beauty. It's a reminder that God sees us—everything in the world—and calls it *good*.

> *God saw everything that [God] had made, and indeed, it was very good.* (Genesis 1:31a)

It isn't an accident that this is the first story in the Bible. So let's pause and reflect on a different verse from the same chapter in Genesis:

> *God created humankind in [God's] image.* (Genesis 1:27a)

You might be thinking: "Oh, great! I've heard this one before. Why are we pausing here? What more could I possibly learn from these seven words which—hey, don't think I didn't notice—*aren't even the entire verse?*"

First, your mind is sharp and wonderful.

Second, these words are the building blocks for a theological concept called *imago Dei*, or the idea that humans have been created in the *image* of God. Our moral, spiritual, and intellectual natures are unique characteristics that point to the divine nature of God. It's God, found inside of us. It's our ability to love deeply, to create fantastically, to live lives that are introspective—to follow God and search for ways to transform ourselves, the entire world.

It's the desire to draw closer to God.

Another way to think about this is that God's self-actualization comes through humanity.

It's okay. You can say it: *"What in the . . . ?"*

Those unique characteristics that humans share? That's a way to see and understand God a little better.

Theologian Jürgen Moltmann believed that we should think about the *imago Dei* as a starting point for how we act—how we carry out God's work in the world. Moltmann believed we were all a work in progress, moving toward our original *imago Dei* status that was found in the Garden of Eden.

Jürgen Moltmann (b.1926) is a theologian who is best known for books such as *Theology of Hope* and *The Crucified God*. Moltmann's theology says that God suffers *with* humanity, while simultaneously promising humanity a future that is ultimately hopeful—something guaranteed by Christ's resurrection. His time in World War II and a single question—*Why did I survive?*—haunted him and were a starting point for much of his theology.

Creationism isn't just a wacky view held by people who don't believe in science and like to make theme parks with names like Creation Land, complete with life-sized versions of Noah's ark and a bunch of hilarious anti-dinosaur "facts."

Yes, it's easy to dunk on that sort of kitsch—to write it off. But know that a theology of creation can also point us to God in beautiful, life-changing ways.

That doesn't mean it isn't without problems.

On the most basic level, the first question we must ask is: If God created the world and everything in it, does that mean that God also created evil? Or if God made order out of chaos, does that means God also created chaos? And if not, was there something before . . . God? And even if we somehow make it through that gauntlet of Big Questions, we'll eventually have to ask whether God sees evil, pain, and grief as *necessary* to how the world functions—to what it means to be human. To quote Abraham: "Shall not the Judge of all the earth do what is just?" (Genesis 18:25).

It goes deeper, too—isn't this fun?

Hey, here's another term that is guaranteed to get your priest, pastor, or youth director looking at you with a combination of respect, suspicion, and low-key horror: *creation ex nihilo.*

Creation ex nihilo is the idea that God created the world from nothing. Again, if you are of the theological stripe that doesn't put much stock in the biblical creation story, the good news here is . . . this isn't going to bother you! However, for much of orthodox Christianity, this question is one to keep you up at night.

The concern is that, if God is the creator and ultimate source of everything in the universe, God is *the source of everything in the universe.* The way most people respond to this (dodge it?) is by saying we all have free will—the freedom to make good and bad choices—so, how can God be blamed for the fact that somebody wants to, say, drive a monster truck to school, the environment be damned? The response to *that* would be—well, why did God create such freedom (or: why did God create monster trucks?) and wouldn't God know that we would misuse it?

Free will means that you can choose any number of possible courses of action in any number of instances. And no matter what you choose— good, bad, completely heinous—you will be able to do so *completely unimpeded* by God. You might be thinking: *Hey, that's kind of a useful theological trick.* And you would be right. When in doubt, look for *Free Will.*

The point here isn't to freak you out.

Please don't freak out.

The point is to show that these questions you might have are baked into the system, so to speak. From page one of the Bible.

If we turn a couple pages in Genesis, we get to the story of Adam and Eve. (Hey! Look! It's another creation story!) You might be thinking, "Great! I remember this story from when I was a kid! What could *possibly* be problematic with the story of the first people?!"

Ahem.

Well.

Let's just do this, Band-Aid style.

The "Abrahamic religions" (Judaism, Islam, and Christianity, all of which share the story of Abraham in the Bible) point to Genesis—specifically, the story of Adam and Eve—to explain the origins of the world as well as what is commonly called "the Fall." It's important to note here that "the Fall" is an *interpretation* of the story, not something that is actually *in* the story. Anyway, the Fall, also called the Fall of Humanity or the Fall of Adam (more on that in a minute), is a term that Christianity often uses to explain why sin is a part of the world.

Now, whether it does a *good* job of explaining this is an open question, and one that we'll come to shortly.

But first, let's unpack Adam and Eve.

The doctrine of the Fall of Humanity comes from the story found in Genesis 3. In this story—we can use the word *myth*, too—we see God creating Adam and Eve, the first two humans. God gives them a home! The Garden of Eden! This is literal paradise. Everything one could want. And it only has one rule: *do not eat from the tree of the knowledge of good and evil.*

This is where the story gets a little . . . weird. Or weirder, let's face it.

Suddenly there's a talking snake and this snake is a *trickster* who's about to really mess things up for

Adam and, specifically, Eve. Because the snake? Well, it starts whispering in Eve's ear, like some kind of strange hype . . . snake.

Tell me exactly what God said.

God surely didn't say what you think.

No, no, no—you aren't going to die.

C'mon, what's the worst that could happen?

You get the idea.

> Snakes and serpents are not always evil, or even bad. (And *not the devil*, in this particular story.) In other religions, myths, and legends of the ancient Near East, the "home" of the Bible and Christianity, snakes and serpents are signs of wisdom, fertility, life, and healing. Even in the Bible, in the book of Exodus, the staffs of Aaron and Moses turn into snakes—a useful trick in the moment!

(And if you *really* want to get into this whole theodicy thing, we probably need to ask why God would let a talking trickster serpent into the garden and whether God *knew* this all was going to happen and . . . well, let's save that mess for later in the book.)

Anyway, the serpent "tempts" Eve, and she decides to eat from the forbidden tree and then shares it with Adam, who in all honesty gets off pretty dang easy in this story.

But c'mon.

You *know* that guy was like, "Oh? Fruit from that forbidden tree? I've had my eye on that tree, for sure. *What could go wrong?*"

The truth is: Eve gets saddled with the *actual sin of the world* and even though some people call it the Fall of Adam, even that title *still* makes it seem like Adam is blameless in this whole story, which is just some B.S.

Anyway. Back to the story.

Suddenly, Adam and Eve realize they're naked and decide to make some clothes, to hide from God, and it only gets worse from there. God kicks them out of the Garden of Eden, takes away eternal life, and tells Eve she's going to have pain now whenever she gives birth. The story ends with God putting some angels with fiery swords in front of the Garden, which, all things considered, is a pretty metal thing to do.

Bonus: Top Five Badass Moments of the Bible (in no particular order)

1. *II Kings 2:23–24*, in which Elisha is just trying to go up to Bethel when some *youths* start making fun of his bald head and he's just not having it so he calls down a curse *in the name of the Lord* and a couple of bears rumble out of the woods and maul—*maul*—forty-two of the youths. A bald youth pastor favorite.

---

2. *Judges 3:16–23*, in which Ehud sneaks in a special sword when he goes to see the king of Moab, "who was a very fat man." Long story short, Ehud tells the king he has a message from God but then—surprise!—plunges the sword into the fat belly of the king. When he pulls his hand out, the sword is gone—still inside the king. So Ehud is like, well I'm out. And leaves the sword *inside the king.*

3. *Judges 15:15–16*, in which Samson makes asses out of his enemies by totally whooping on them with an ass's jawbone. (Shout out to Balaam's talking ass as another contender for best donkey in the Bible.)

4. *Judges 4:22*, in which Jael pretends to be friendly with an enemy general but then saves the day by driving a tent stake through the dude's *head.*

5. *Revelation 9:6*, in which we find a verse that isn't about zombies but still sounds like it's kind of about zombies: "And in those days people will seek death but will not find it; they will long to die, but death will flee from them."

Now, there are a few issues we should deal with. First, was this Eve's fault?

No.

Stories, sacred myths such as this one, are typically used to make sense of a particular situation or problem the community is facing. More often than not, assumptions about gender, sexuality—any number of things—can be assigned to a story or myth because they are assumed to be universally true. While opinions vary on whether anything can be *universally* true for all people, let's say—for the purposes of this conversation—that it's always important to ask questions of scripture, to investigate how certain stories came into being and analyze who has the power and who does not, who stands to gain from the story as it is told.

> Culturally, we've turned the word *myth* into something that is the same as a lie. But in this sense, it's inaccurate. A *sacred myth* allows us to hear stories—mine them for truth and meaning—without having to continually stumble over illogical or unscientific elements. So, are Bible stories history? Some are. Most are not.

So, it wasn't Eve's fault. And—get ready, friends—we should probably mention that this story isn't *literally true.* Instead, it helps its intended audience understand the world better. It's true in a way that's bigger than facts. With that said, does it make sense to claim that women are to blame for the Fall of Humanity? The original cause of sin?

Answer that one yourself.

This story was used to develop the theological concept of *original sin*. Original sin, sometimes called first sin, is a way to explain—again, usually unhelpfully!—why the world seems so crappy, so broken. Why bad things happen. Adam and Eve ate that fruit, which introduced sin and death to the world. And now we suffer the consequences.

Original sin is an easy and, for some, tidy way to answer the question of evil and suffering. However, much like other pat answers for why bad things happen, original sin is often used as a sort of cover-all answer. Something that, when we don't have an answer, becomes . . . the answer.

Is there a compelling reason to believe that sin is a part of the world? Yes. We see it every day. It is in fact the reason for writing (and maybe reading) this book. But *sin* is a loaded word! Something that immediately triggers all kinds of *feelings*.

So, let's spend a few moments on sin.

Sin, most broadly defined, is separation from God.

This can look a lot of different ways. It's been interpreted as what we can and cannot eat, how we speak about God, arrogance, and, unfortunately, simply being the person that God created you to be (which, let's just clear it up now, is not sinful). The list goes on and on. Sin can be considered *personal* or *actual*, which is usually separated from *original sin*, sins we can (again, maybe?) avoid—sins that are a result of our free will.

Now, depending on your particular flavor of Christianity, this is where it gets a little more complicated and starts involving concepts like *redemption* and *atonement*, which are both words that try to figure out what happened to Jesus—and why—and how it all works when it comes to the sin of the world.

That, friends, is a totally different book and a totally different can of worms. And since we're crawling with theological worms right now, let's do a couple quick definitions and move on.

Redemption: As simply as possible, this is the deliverance from sin. You may have heard people talk about being "saved," which is often loaded, exclusive, and unhelpful language, but what they're actually talking about is the work of God in the world—dealing with sin and understanding the mechanics of what we call *salvation*.

Atonement: The work of being reconciled to God, usually seen through Christ's death and resurrection. This is where you see a lot of language about *lambs* and *blood* and terrible t-shirts with pictures of Jesus nailed to the cross with completely ridiculous sayings like "Body piercing saved my life." Atonement theories are plentiful. A lot of them are awful and actively separate us from the idea of a loving God. But the good ones remind us that God is seeking reconciliation in the world. That God *wants* us.

Okay, back to sin.

Now, thinking about sin as both a corrupted nature (original sin) and the crappy things we sometimes do to one another (personal/actual sin) isn't all bad. Sin language can be a powerful word to disrupt injustice, to call out people and systems that prey on marginalized people—those who are not in power and cannot protect themselves.

The Episcopal Baptismal Covenant (promises made by or on behalf of the person being baptized) talks about evil/sin on three levels—cosmic, worldy, and personal. It's a complete renunciation of sin and evil, big and small, in all parts of our lives—a commitment to naming, confronting, and acting against evil in all forms. But it's also an acknowledgment that we're going to mess up—we're going to sin! When that happens, we repent—we turn around; we return—and are reconciled with God.

The problem, of course, is that sin can ultimately become *very* subjective. A good guide for those who claim Christianity is Jesus himself. What did Jesus consider sinful? What did Jesus speak about? That list is often surprising and just as challenging (see: a camel going through the eye of a needle).

"Again I tell you, it is easier for a camel to go through the eye of a needle than for someone who is rich to enter the kingdom of God." (Matthew 19:24)

If you ever find yourself stressing out about whether something is a sin, find peace and hope in the fact that

Jesus always chooses people and their specific contexts over monolithic religious "rules."

Fine, that's all well and good, but what does it *mean*?

Well, if somebody is dead set on telling you something is a sin . . . there's a context involved, a theological point of view that makes them believe that *x* is sinful. It is never wrong to ask questions, to challenge contexts. And if people don't like it, well, you're in good company. Jesus was all about reversing expectations and making things new.

So perhaps we're back to where we started—separation from God.

That feels right . . . and it brings us back to the story of Adam and Eve.

They heard the sound of the Lord God walking in the garden at the time of the evening breeze, and the man and his wife hid themselves from the presence of the Lord God among the trees of the garden. But the Lord God called to the man, and said to him, "Where are you?" (Genesis 3:8–9)

Adam and Eve are hiding from God—they're embarrassed, perhaps worried. They are separated from God, despite being in God's presence. Admittedly, it's not a perfect illustration. However, the story of Adam and Eve is a powerful reminder that our transgressions (speaking of not wanting to use sin language!) may come with consequences, but they do not necessarily define how we will be perceived—how we will continue to be deeply loved and known, despite our mistakes.

More importantly, this section of the story reminds us that one of the reasons we still talk about sin is that it reminds us of the pain, the sickness, the hurt that we all feel. It's a reminder that we can bring that pain, those questions, even holy rage, to God because God isn't out there patrolling the world waiting for us to mess up. Instead, God is calling out to us—*Where are you?*—beckoning us closer.

Some may interpret this to be a story of shame, removing all the space for the blessing of being sought out—of being found. Can you justify such a reading? Sure. But what a small and sad picture of God.

Instead, consider it an invitation to be messy. To not have all the answers. To know that—even when you do screw up, when you try to hide from God—the response is not going to be the divine cold shoulder.

This is starting to sound an awful lot like one of those church camp nights when everybody circles up and holds hands and suddenly some youth director breaks out an acoustic guitar and the whole group is doing that camp call-and-response thing—*God is good . . . ALL THE TIME!*

There's nothing wrong with camp or even call-and-responses (but the acoustic guitar might be one of those *cosmic evils* the Baptismal Covenant warns us about . . .).

In all seriousness, you might have noticed that we skipped a couple of big questions.

Most notably, wouldn't it just be easier to *not* believe in any of this?

Sin. Original sin. Adam and Eve.

Why not toss all of it?

And while we're on the subject, what if God—just spitballing here—simply *fixed everything* for us?

That would be a great solution, right?

Let's take them one at a time.

First things first. Well, *yeah*.

There are a lot of people who simply do not include sin as a part of their theological worldview. In some ways, this is another one of those easy fixes—but this one comes with some sensible reasons. Original sin, frankly, is what is called a "theological construct," meaning that it is never explicitly referred to in the Bible. God does not—if you recall—say, "You have now committed ORIGINAL SIN. I am so sorry. Please exit the Garden of Eden."

The first ideas around this came in the fourth century from Augustine, who quickly tied the story of Adam and Eve not only to original sin but decided to really go for it and classify it as *sinful lust*.

He was really fun at parties.

Basically, Augustine taught that human sexuality was corrupted at the Fall and could not be redeemed until the final resurrection of the body. And, just to put an extra special cherry on top of everything, Augustine was the first to introduce *inherited guilt* from Adam.

What's that? See that sweet baby over there who couldn't possibly have done *anything wrong*, well, Augustine is sorry to tell you that baby is *eternally damned* at birth.

Yep, fun at parties.

Augustine of Hippo. Born 354 CE; died 430 CE. Theologian. Philosopher. Bishop in North Africa. His writings—perhaps more than any other—influenced the development of not only the church but also Western philosophy. Pronounced Augus-*tin*. Not Augus-*teen*. Famous works include *Confessions*, *The City of God*, and *On Christian Doctrine*.

Naturally, there were (and still are!) theologians who don't jibe with Augustine's point of view. More recently, theologians have insisted that the concept of original sin was never a part of Jesus's worldview or that of the early church. The argument goes: original sin is not helpful because we all know that evil exists—we know that bad things happen!

God created the world not for separation, but for relationship. A deep connection between humanity and the divine. So, on its face, sin is incompatible with the idea of God. How could we ever truly be separated? This is rooted in the never-ending, ongoing, bigger-than-you-can-imagine love of God. It says that, yeah, you're going to screw up, but what's more important than that screwup is that you are still loved. Without hesitation. Without qualification.

God loves you. No matter what. And *nothing* you can do will change that fact.

Beloved is our starting place.

If that's the case, why doesn't God just fix it?

Well, that's a question that will result in heavy coughing, nervous pacing, a sudden case of the sweats, followed by a mumbled explanation that includes words like "free will" and "subordination" and, let's face it, we've already been through a lot, so let's just admit that *we actually don't know why* God doesn't just fix everything for us.

This, of course, hasn't stopped a lot of people from trying.

The (Mostly) Dead Theologians Answer Club

A PLAY IN ONE ACT

Dramatis personae
Moderator
Pelagius
Augustine
Gottfried Leibniz
Irenaeus
Origen
Friedrich Schleiermacher
Max Weber
Karl Marx
Georg Wilhelm Friedrich Hegel
Immanuel Kant
Emilie Townes
Thomas Aquinas
Kelly Brown Douglas

Delores Williams
Twitter Theology Guy
The Process Party
Monica Coleman
Jürgen Moltmann
Zachary Braiterman
C. S. Lewis
Karl Barth

A large lecture hall. At the front sits a collection of, let's admit it, fairly weird and anxious-looking people. These are theologians. Philosophers. All of them seem to be haunted by questions that we cannot see. You will meet them individually; collectively, they are The Group.

This will certainly be the most fun you've ever had.

MODERATOR

Welcome to . . . The (Mostly) Dead Theologians Answer Club, where we come to discuss the biggest problems that face humanity from a theological and philosophical lens. Today we will be discussing . . . THEODICY.

PELAGIUS*

There is no such thing.

---

*Pelagius was a theologian who lived from 360 CE to 420 CE and believed that humans had the "moral ability" to not sin. His theology, called Pelagianism, led to him being designated not simply a heretic, but an *arch-heretic*, which means you've likely upset a few people.

AUGUSTINE*

Don't make me cancel you again.

MODERATOR

Friends, let's take a big breath. Okay, are we ready?
*(The Group nods, already seemingly
at odds with one another.)*

MODERATOR *(continuing)*

Okay, let's turn first to our friend Gottfried Leibniz, who coined the term "theodicy" in an attempt to justify God's existence in light of all the evil we see.

LEIBNIZ†

Thank you, in this lecture I will begin by—

AUGUSTINE

I object! I spoke about this way before Gottfried, here. He may have come up with the word, but give credit where credit is due.

PELAGIUS

And without me, my friend Gus would not have even done that, so give credit where—

---

*You've already met Augustine of Hippo (-tin not -teen), but it's worth noting that Augustine was having *none* of Pelagius and wrote about him . . . often.
†Gottfried Wilhelm Leibniz (1646 to 1716) not only had a fabulous name but was a mathematician, philosopher, scientist, and diplomat. He also coined the term *theodicy.*

AUGUSTINE

We do not give credit to arch-heretics! And don't call me "Gus."

PELAGIUS

Arch-heretic is a strong word, Gus. I prefer *heterodox*, or one who holds a view outside of the popular belief.

MODERATOR

Okay, let's get this cleared up. Pelagius, would you mind starting us out?

PELAGIUS *(clears throat)*

Well, Pelagianism—

AUGUSTINE

—was basically defined by my critique of it.

MODERATOR

Gentlemen . . .

PELAGIUS

Anyway, that is somewhat true. And Gus has turned it into a bit of a bad word—tossed around anytime some Christian on social media wants to claim heresy.

THE GROUP

What is social media?

MODERATOR

An example of the Fall of Humanity.
(SFX: Zing!)

PELAGIUS

Well, let's just start with a reminder that Pelagianism had *substantial* support among many Christians. Because it makes sense to believe that God could not command humans to do the impossible, so it must be possible to follow all the Commandments.

AUGUSTINE

And that is completely—

PELAGIUS

Also, babies are born blameless and without sin because only a monster would think otherwise.

(*Pelagius stares intently at Augustine.*)

PELAGIUS

So, there was no excuse for sinful behavior. If God thinks we can live sinless lives, then so do I!

(*The Group mumbles.*)

MODERATOR

Thank you, Pelagius. Now, Augustine would you like to—

AUGUSTINE

I'm about to blow this up just like I did in the fourth century, y'all!

MODERATOR

Just make sure you keep it polite.

AUGUSTINE

Pelagius is "the enemy of the grace of God."

MODERATOR
Great. Thank you.

AUGUSTINE *(unaffected)*
We are all corrupted by original sin and we cannot choose good. So sin, all the bad things of the world, are the result—the inevitable result!—of a fallen human nature.
(Augustine mimes dropping a microphone.)

AUGUSTINE *(continuing)*
And that's what they call *orthodoxy*, my friends. So, to recap, God cannot be blamed for evil—God is, in fact, not responsible!
(Augustine mimes his mind being blown.)

MODERATOR
Excellent. Well, there might be some more words on the subject.

AUGUSTINE
Surely not.

MODERATOR
Well, how about we turn to Irenaeus, a second-century theologian who, with the help of John Hick, a philosopher who showed up nearly two thousand years later, developed his own theodicy.

IRENAEUS*

Wait. I did?

MODERATOR

Well, as Augustine contended, humans were created perfect but fell and then became victims of their own free will. You, Irenaeus, believed that humans were not perfect but continue to move toward it.

IRENAEUS

This all makes sense and I—

MODERATOR

And you believed God is responsible for evil but God is *not* at fault for this because evil is, in fact, necessary for the greater good.

(The Group looks around at each other awkwardly.)

IRENAEUS

Well, I mean, um, we can all *see* evil, right? Like, there's evidence of evil in the world. And if an all-powerful, loving God exists, there *shouldn't* be evil in the world. So, what I'm trying to do is show that the existence of God is probable despite the occurrence of evil.

(Silence. Deep, deafening silence.)

---

*Irenaeus (c. 130 CE to c. 202 CE) was a Greek bishop who is widely known for helping define orthodoxy (translated, simply, as "right belief"). He wrote *Against Heresies*, which, you guessed it, is about refuting heresies and establishing . . . orthodoxy. Also likely fun at parties.

IRENAEUS *(nervously)*

Um, but, like, also I want to say that the entire world—all humans—are still in process, a work in progress you could say. First, we were created in the image of God and then the likeness . . . and, uh, we're all still moving toward that likeness.

MODERATOR

That's right! And this is sometimes called the "soul-making theodicy" and leads to the development of Leibniz's "best possible world," which means that evil and suffering would allow humans to develop more completely. Which, as you can imagine, isn't always received well!

ORIGEN*

May I have a word?

MODERATOR

Ah, it's early Christian theologian and scholar Origen. Go ahead!

ORIGEN

Suffering is necessary for the development of all humans. As I like to say, the world is a school and a

---

*Origen of Alexandria (c. 184 CE to c. 253 CE) was a Christian theologian who wrote *a lot*, which was possible because his good friend Ambrose of Alexandria hooked him up with a team of secretaries to copy everything down, making him the Heavyweight Champion of Antiquity Writers (not an officially recognized championship belt).

hospital for the soul. And God is our teacher and physician. So, our suffering teaches us and heals us!
(*Augustine mimes his mind being blown.*)

MODERATOR

Well, how about we move on to a different—

FRIEDRICH SCHLEIERMACHER*

Oh, you *know* I'm about to weigh in on this.

MODERATOR

Dear God, help us.

SCHLEIERMACHER

God is omnipotent. God is benevolent. Does anyone disagree?

(*Nobody disagrees.*)

SCHLEIERMACHER (*continuing*)

So that means that God *must* create flawlessly.
(*Schleiermacher also drops the mic and
receives a fist bump from Augustine.*)

MODERATOR

Well, um . . .

---

*Friedrich Schleiermacher (1768 to 1834), besides having a *great* name, was a German theologian and biblical scholar. He's often called the "Father of Modern Liberal Theology," but let's assume that did not go to his head.

SCHLEIERMACHER

But that also means that everybody will be saved, which is called universalism. It's only logical! Who's with me?!

(Schleiermacher reaches for another fist bump, but Augustine turns away, disgusted.)

MODERATOR

Well, perhaps we should go back to Leibniz because—

MAX WEBER*

Let's go!

MODERATOR

Hey everybody, it's noted philosopher and social critic Max Weber.

WEBER

Well, we all know that theodicy is merely a social theory—something used by different classes of people to explain their specific social situation.

---

*Max Weber (pronounced with a "v"—*vay-ber*) (1864 to 1920) was one of the most important thinkers of the modern era. His work *The Protestant Ethic and the Spirit of Capitalism* tied Protestantism (Christianity that developed outside of the Roman Catholic Church) and capitalism together, saying they shared the same values.

KARL MARX*

Did I hear somebody mention social analysis?

MODERATOR

How did you get in here?

MARX

I'm everywhere. *Everywhere.*

WEBER

It's all about theodicies of fortune and misfortune. Or, if you have a lot of material goods—you might believe that you deserve what you got, because you worked hard for it and God rewarded you.

MARX

Which is ludicrous, comrades.

WEBER

And so a theodicy of misfortune means—

MARX

That wealth and privilege are *actually evil.*

---

*Karl Marx (1818 to 1883) was a writer, philosopher, and social revolutionary who is known for, among other writings, *The Communist Manifesto* and his critique of capitalism. He called religion the "opiate of the masses," which, you can imagine, did not make him a lot of friends during coffee hour at church. But hey, here's a fun fact: his name can be used as an adjective, noun, *and* social theory!

WEBER

Well, I'd say *signs* of evil.

MARX

Did I stutter?

MODERATOR

Well, thank you, Mr. Weber and Mr. Marx—

MARX

I want to clear up the whole "opiate of the masses" thing really quickly, if I may.

MODERATOR

Well, hey! This is a very special opportunity for our audience. Karl Marx, long vilified by some believers, is here to give us further insight into possibly the most well-known and misunderstood quote in all of philosophy. So, go ahead, Mr. Marx.

MARX *(thinking)*

Actually, no. I meant every word of it. LIBERATE YOURSELF FROM THE SYSTEMS OF OPPRESSION! WORKERS UNITED AND—

GEORG WILHELM FRIEDRICH HEGEL*

Is this the right room?

MODERATOR

No. Absolutely not. They'll see you again in college.

(Hegel leaves the room, dejected. Both Weber and Marx excitedly follow.)

MODERATOR *(recovering)*

Okay. I think it's time for a quick recap. We have Irenaeus's soul-making theodicy, Augustine's free will argument, Leibniz's best-of-all-possible-worlds explanation, so before we turn to some of our more modern guests, we can—

LEIBNIZ

Actually, I have more to say. Reason and faith need to be reconciled with one another. They are both gifts from God. And if we were to reject one to make the other easier to understand, we are committing a grievous error. So, our current world *has* to be a perfect world. This *has* to be the answer to the question of evil!

---

*Georg Wilhelm Friedrich Hegel (1770 to 1831) took a mean selfie (look him up) and also happened to be one of the most influential figures in Western philosophy. Despite his writings being deeply challenging, he spawned a devoted group of followers called the Young Hegelians, which you *know* had to be a wild group of kids and, not for nothing, would also make an excellent band name.

IMMANUEL KANT*

Entering the chat to say *no.*

MODERATOR

Hey! It's Immanuel Kant, one of the most prominent philosophers of all time!

LEIBNIZ

Surely you must agree that there are unavoidable limitations in being human, which lead to our problems—*right?*

KANT

Oh yes. That is not up for debate. But I would suggest that many of the answers here are nothing but apologies that ultimately, when considered for more than a few seconds, are worse than the charges we currently are leveling against God.

(Kant, after finishing, abruptly leaves the room.)

MODERATOR

Uh, Immanuel Kant, everybody . . .

(The MODERATOR composes themself,
clearing their throat.)

---

*Immanuel Kant (1724 to 1804) was a philosopher and one of the central thinkers of the Enlightenment era. He is known for the *categorical imperative*, which is a universal principle that states there are certain mandatory moral laws that everyone has the duty to follow.

MODERATOR *(continuing)*

Now, let's bring ourselves into a more modern place when it comes to thinking through these questions. Let's acknowledge that the conversation has been dominated by a lot of dead dudes and so these *very alive* theologians—who all promise to understand that this is *not* a complete reflection of their great work and simply a very, very fun bit—will help us to see how big and wonderful theology can be when everyone is included. Which is a good reminder that theology requires us to realize who is talking and who isn't allowed to talk, who is in the room and who hasn't been let inside.

EMILIE TOWNES

That was quite the caveat.

MODERATOR

Please, nobody sue us.

EMILIE TOWNES*

Anyway, I think this might be a good time to introduce you to the idea of womanist theology.

---

*Emilie Townes (b. 1955) is a womanist theologian and the first Black woman to be elected president of the American Academy of Religion. She is an ordained American Baptist Minister and a prolific writer and thinker.

MODERATOR

Good idea, Emilie Townes! And hey, we should mention that you're one of the most important Black theologians of this century!

TOWNES

Womanist theology—which is a theology by and for Black women—looks at theodicy a little differently. We are not concerned with using the typical theological problems, such as figuring out how God is involved.

MODERATOR

Ohh . . . interesting! This is very helpful.

TOWNES

Instead, we ask how humans have failed to live as full partners with God. We ask how we can have better relationships with one another. By doing this, we refuse to let evil or suffering have the last word. We refuse to believe in a small God.

AQUINAS*

But what about . . . *theology!*

---

*Thomas Aquinas (1225 to 1274) was an Italian theologian, a Catholic priest, and one of the most influential theologians ever. In fact, much of Western philosophy and theology, in one way or another, is either building on his ideas or actively trying to refute them. His best-known work is *Summa Theologica*.

TOWNES

We do theology. But we don't limit ourselves to dead white guys or traditional understandings of what sources of theology might look like. So, instead of reading—well, you—we also look at gospel music, sexuality, African spirituality, poetry, and literature as ways to understand God better. All of these are important sources of truth!

AQUINAS

Well. I guess I'll sit down now.

MODERATOR

Thomas Aquinas, everybody—who, basically, just extended Augustine's view of theodicy and didn't really make things better for us . . .

       (The MODERATOR pauses, looks
       sideways, and then . . .)

MODERATOR

Anyway!

KELLY BROWN DOUGLAS*

Hey, we should also talk about womanist theology's responsibility to poor and working-class Black women.

---

*The Rev. Dr. Kelly Brown Douglas is a womanist theologian, Episcopal priest, and dean of the Episcopal Divinity School. She was one of the first ten Black women to be ordained in the Episcopal Church.

MARX *(sticking his head into the room)*
Did I hear somebody say my name?

GROUP
No!

(Marx slowly retreats from view.)

MODERATOR
Hey, it's Kelly Brown Douglas, a noted academic and priest in the Episcopal Church!

DOUGLAS
Right, so what point is any of this talk about theodicy if people outside of the academy aren't going to be affected by it?

MODERATOR
The "academy" is basically college, kids. It's full of dusty old books and dustier old professors who, sometimes, are having a conversation that is so outside the bounds of normal people that, well, it's just—

DOUGLAS
It's not accountable to the church. And as a result, it doesn't empower the people it hopes to empower. For womanist theology, that means Black women. Basically, we need to hear their experiences and get their opinions on these questions.

DELORES WILLIAMS*

Right. And if we're going to ever talk about salvation, then we *need* to make sure that it addresses the suffering and evil that Black women experience.

MODERATOR

Ah, Delores Williams—one of the prominent voices in womanist theology! She reminds us that sin is very much a social thing, something that one group of people often inflicts on another group of people.

WILLIAMS

But we can combat evil and suffering—we can actually address salvation by *participating* in work against it.

PELAGIUS

This sounds like my kind of party.

WILLIAMS

I don't know about that, but sin and salvation are definitely not found in one act. And salvation is the process of working together to alleviate the sins (and the sinful behavior) of the world!

---

*Delores Williams (b. 1937) is one of the pioneers of womanist theology. The term *womanist* was coined by her contemporary Alice Walker, author of *The Color Purple*. Williams is best known for her book *Sisters in the Wilderness*.

MODERATOR

You said . . . *process.* I think now would be a great time to invite another womanist theologian—and not to mention a *process theologian*—Monica Coleman!*

(Before Monica Coleman can stand up and speak, the doors of the lecture hall burst open and a stream of wildly dressed people—lampshades on their heads, the whole bit—come dancing into the room. They seem unruly. Possibly dangerous. But they do look like they're having a good time.)

MODERATOR

Hey! Look! It's the Process (theology) Party!†

TWITTER THEOLOGY GUY

Actually, that's #processparty.

---

*Rev. Dr. Monica Coleman is a scholar, writer, and theologian who is known for her work in process and womanist theologies. She is ordained in the African Methodist Episcopal Church and has written six books.

†Process Party or #processparty is a social media phenomenon where like-minded theologians—or those who are interested in process theology, generally speaking—will have conversations about, well, process theology. So, it's not so much a party as it's . . . well, it's just not a party at all. But it's fun? For, like, theology and stuff? Think memes, people expanding what it means to follow God, and the occasional mansplaining theology guy who quickly gets muted. #processparty!

MODERATOR

Anyway! Monica Coleman!

MONICA COLEMAN

We are all interdependent with one another, which means if one of us operates in a way that's antithetical to God's calling, it affects all of us! This is where process theology becomes critical. It helps us think about God and evil in ways that don't contradict, well, everything else we know about the world.

MODERATOR

Why yes, process theology seems like a great answer to many of these problems, doesn't it! We're talking about essential kenosis!* That's a fancy term that allows God to be *almighty* while also acknowledging that God can't prevent *genuine* or, as Kant might call it, *radical evil*. God can't—and won't!—override our decisions or fail to give us the capacity to have freedom. Self-choice! So, God can't be blamed!

MONICA COLEMAN

I'd frame it slightly differently and describe it as God "making a way out of no way." It suggests that there are possibilities we can't comprehend—that the way forward isn't contained in ways that are already "known."

Kenosis is the "self-emptying" of Jesus Christ's human or personal will in order to be completely in tune with God's divine will. Check out Philippians 2:7 for a relevant Bible verse.

Instead, God presents us with possibilities that will increase our quality of life from multiple sources.

MODERATOR

And in your work, you also remind us that a theodicy should not only increase quality of life but also make survival and justice a goal.

COLEMAN

Yes! And it should challenge the existing order and power structures!

MODERATOR

This reminds me that, for many people, process theology is helpful because it can "solve" the problem of evil—theodicy. It tells us that God, too, suffers. God changes God's mind. It says that we all are a part of the beautiful process of creating!

JÜRGEN MOLTMANN

Well, there are other people who talk about a suffering God. I'm just saying.

MODERATOR

Ah! Yes, Dr. Moltmann! You developed an idea of the Suffering God based on your time spent in a prisoner of war camp during World War II.

MOLTMANN

Well, I also believe that God suffers alongside and with humanity, which is a big deal because it means that

God is not *impassible*—or that God is not above feel-ings! This is huge! But perhaps the biggest thing I can add to this conversation is that the suffering is not meaningless.

ORIGEN

Oh yeah. Back in the game!

MOLTMANN

Well . . . I cannot say that suffering in itself is meaning-ful, or that it is warranted.

ORIGEN

Annnnnnd I'm out.

MOLTMANN

But the promise from God comes in the form of *hope*, which we receive through the resurrection of Jesus.

MODERATOR

You could call that . . . a theology of hope.

MOLTMANN

You could! And I did!

MODERATOR

I think we would be remiss if we didn't bring in some different voices at this time—some of our friends from the Jewish faith.

ZACHARY BRAITERMAN*

Well, I guess I'm up. I'm not really into theodicy. I'd rather talk about *anti-theodicy*.

THE GROUP

Ooohhh.

MODERATOR

Zachary Braiterman is a Jewish theologian who wrote a book called *(God) After Auschwitz*, where his response to evil was to protest the connection between it and God—similar to Job!

BRAITERMAN

I wasn't the first Jewish theologian or philosopher to consider this. Emmanuel Levinas considered theodicy "blasphemous" because humans aren't supposed to justify God—but to live better lives!

PELAGIUS

I'm just sayin' . . .

MODERATOR

I think an *anti-theodicy* could, perhaps, become a theology that focuses on things we *do* understand and

---

*Zachary Braiterman (b. 1963) is a philosopher who writes about Holocaust theology and Jewish thought. He is best known for refusing to connect the horrors of the Holocaust with God. As a result, he coined the term *anti-theodicy*.

control. Perhaps one focused around community, about culture. How we engage those things!

BRAITERMAN

And not everybody agrees with me in Jewish theology circles. Some believe that rejecting God gives Hitler a victory. Others blame free will for God remaining hidden.

AUGUSTINE

Ahem.

BRAITERMAN

And then there is the idea that, maybe, God is not omnipotent or omniscient, which means there is no contradiction between a good God and the atrocity of the Holocaust.

PROCESS PARTY

What-*what!*

MODERATOR

And then there's Elie Wiesel, who doesn't want to come out on a clear answer! It's a sort of existential pro-test, which will not deny God but also does not accept theodicies.

BRAITERMAN

I just want to say that an *anti-theodicy* rejects any idea that there is a meaningful relationship between God and evil or that God could be justified for the experience of evil.

MODERATOR

Well, this has been quite a session of The (Mostly) Dead Theologians Answer Club. I think we've covered a lot of ground, so until next time—

C. S. LEWIS

Hold on there. I wrote a *lot* about suffering and grief!

KARL BARTH*

Uh, and I think I should have something to say, namely that God's suffering on the cross makes any and all human theodicies anticlimactic!

C. S. LEWIS†

But seriously. *Grief Observed. The Problem of Pain.* Google me, people. This is outrageous.

---

*Karl Barth is one of the most prominent theologians of the twentieth century. He is best known for his *Commentary on the Book of Romans* as well as his (unfinished, but massive) multivolume theological treatise *Church Dogmatics.* He was, and remains, a Big Deal.
†Clive Staples Lewis (1898 to 1963) not only has a name that sounds like he's a saxophone player in a really hot blues band but also is one of the most prominent religious writers of the twentieth century. He wrote popular theology books, as well as *The Chronicles of Narnia* (seriously: Google the man), and is a great example of a person who allowed his faith to profoundly affect his life and work—often in ways that surprised even old Clive.

MODERATOR

Well, it's impossible to truly get insights from every person who's ever spoken about theodicy because, frankly, it's something we all deal with! We all have our own answers!

MARX

If I may . . .

MODERATOR

Well, looks like that's the end of the show! Until next time . . . keep the theodicies coming and don't let the existential threat of the problem of evil get you down!

A Necessary Interlude

Okay. You look like you could use . . .

    A Necessary Interlude!

Let's check in for a second.

How are you feeling? What are you thinking about?

It might be helpful to grab a pen or pencil and a piece of paper and just let go—journal, free-form, and see what comes out.

Because: this is . . . a lot.

And more than likely, you've been through . . . things.

These *things* could be big or small. (Remember: the size of our pain or grief doesn't really matter, because our theodicies are first and foremost *individual*—they answer and help us process personal tragedies, as well as bigger issues we notice and experience.) So sometimes when we start scratching at the surface of a question—especially a big question like this one—we realize that there's a bigger hole there than we thought.

So, take your time with this.

Give yourself some grace, some room to put this book down and come back to it later.

We'll be here.

The important thing is that the point of this book—of asking these sorts of questions—is not to produce harm but to draw you into a closer, more meaningful relationship with God.

Or you could be thinking, "Oh heck no. *Bring it on.*"

And if that's the case, good! That's just as valid a response! (As is "My priest/pastor is making me read this and I couldn't stop even if I wanted to *thank you very much.*")

Anyway. Say this sort of discussion gets you excited. Like, you can't sit still because you can just *feel* the new ideas rattling around in your brain.

What sparks your curiosity? Where are you finding new energy? A fresh perspective?

You guessed it. Grab that pen or pencil and your favorite notebook! Write that mess out! See what you come up with!

Because we are building something here.

Or to use a word that has some definite theological connotations—we're *constructing* something. Constructive theology is different from what is called *systematic theology*. In systematic theology, the theologian is looking to create a singular, coherent theology that answers all questions about God—specifically the "big" ones in the Christian tradition, such as doctrines around Jesus, salvation, the Holy Spirit, the nature of God . . . sin and theodicy. The problem with this, typically, has been that theologians focus on making the *system* work while sometimes forgetting the bigger goal . . . which is to understand ourselves and God a little better.

Constructive theology looks to redefine this idea. Led in part by Christian feminist theologians such as Sallie McFague and Catherine Keller, constructive theology hopes to defy any expectations of theology! It's a "you know it when you see it" type of theology. Constructive theology implies a certain openness, a flexibility with *how* we come to different answers—to different questions.

Sallie McFague (1933 to 2019) was a prominent feminist theologian who is best known for discussing how metaphors help us understand God better—specifically when it comes to discussing and analyzing ecological issues.

Catherine Keller (b. 1953) is a process (party!) theologian who also works with both feminist and ecological issues, showing how God is relationally involved with the world.

All we're saying is: expect a little dust.

This is just another set of tools to make sure that you create a foundation for future construction and future growth.

So, check in with yourself again. Has your breathing returned to normal? Is that pulse back down to a normal resting rate? Good. Before you jump into the next section—and I know you cannot *wait* to see what we're talking about—take a second to remind yourself of your place in God's world.

Read—pray, even—through this verse from the Letter of Paul to the Romans:

> *For I am convinced that neither death, nor life, nor angels, nor rulers, nor things present, nor things to come, nor powers, nor height, nor depth, nor anything else in all creation, will be able to separate us from the love of God in Christ Jesus our Lord.* (8:38–39)

Hear that you are loved.

Hear that nothing can keep you separated from God.

Not death or sin or whatever happens in our lives.

Nothing.

And now think about how *huge* of a word that is . . .

Nothing.

Nothing can separate us from the love of God.

Not heights or depths.

Not theodicies or books that your pastor/priest might make you read.

Not even bad jokes.

Nothing.

Spend a few minutes placing yourself into God's view of you. See yourself as God sees you—beloved. Created in God's image and called good.

I am fearfully and wonderfully made. (Psalm 139:14)

5

Are You There, God? It's Me... and I Have a Lot of Questions

If you hang around in churches long enough (or, you know, read a dollar bill) somebody's going to say something like "Trust God."

I mean, it sounds like good advice—right?

But how do we *know* that we should trust God?

This question hits even harder when you're facing real pain or grief. How do we *know* that God isn't sitting wherever it is that God sits (brief digression here, but *does* God sit?), choosing whether to act on a prayer of intercession for a good grade on your chemistry exam but also, like, preventing car accidents and illness and . . . well, you get the idea.

Trust God? Cool, cool.

But how do we *know*?

Luckily, we have a few tools at our disposal for answering this question. But let's not get too excited. Like much of theology, the *answers* can seem like a weird foreign film that's been discounted a hundred times and is now sitting by itself in the clearance bin—interesting, but potentially unfulfilling. But unlike, say, *Thomas Cranmer and Vida Scudder versus the Aliens*, we have a pretty interesting investigation into who God is and how God acts.

This is what you call *religious humor*. So, if you're wondering why you didn't get the joke there's a very good reason. Still. You should know these people. **Thomas Cranmer** (1489 to 1556) wrote and compiled the first two versions of the Book of Common Prayer. (He also worked with Henry VIII to annul a marriage, but . . . look it up). **Vida Dutton Scudder** (1861 to 1954) was—in all senses of the word—totally radical. A writer and activist, she was a socialist, a prominent lesbian author, who was dedicated to finding ways to combine her deep spirituality with her commitment to justice. The aliens? That's the joke.

First, let's acknowledge that the whole reason we're in this mess is because we believe that God is good and loving! And depending on your faith tradition (or lack of one), you might also believe that God is all-knowing and all-powerful. Again, this isn't inherently bad theology.

But it's also kind of the problem. It's the literal questions we're trying to answer.

What do we do?

First, let's tackle what are considered the "classic" attributes of God. These are sometimes called the *omnis*, as they refer to the idea that God is *omniscient* (all-knowing; you can add *omnificent*, or the ability to create freely, here as well), *omnipotent* (all-powerful), and *omnipresent* (everywhere at all times). The prefix *omni* means "all, universality." It's supposed to be something that *should* serve as a comfort to us—a God who is totally, completely in control. Naturally, there are ways of arguing for and against that idea—as we've seen—but know that when you start talking about the *omnis*, you are inching closer to the edge that gets people standing up and yelling words like "Heresy!" and "Tie that person to a stake and get some kindling!" (Okay, hopefully we're past the whole "burn heretics at the stake" part of Christianity, but know that's a part of our history!) For some theologians, the *omnis* are *clearly* taught in scripture and to deny (or perhaps even question!) any of them is to deny the God of the Bible. On the other hand, there are plenty of theologians who look at the *omnis* and think, *Wellllll, let's move on.*

You can already see where this is going. But stick with it for a second.

This sort of inflexible theology—we're trying not to say bad, but listen, it's not great theology—comes from a *very particular* point of view of God that is ultimately uncomfortable with a God who changes or has the capacity to surprise us (which is totally supported in scripture, by the way—hello, Noah and the flood!)

So, Noah. You know some vague version of this story. Basically, God is like, Hey, Noah, the world is a *mess*. Full of wickedness and corruption and violence. And Noah is like, OH CRAP GOD IS TALKING TO ME. (Okay, not *really*, but that's probably how it went down.) Anyway. God is like, Build a boat, I'm about to flood *everything* and start over. Even gives Noah *plans* for a boat—an ark. Tells him he can bring his kids, his wife, his sons' wives. And yeah—two of every animal. Noah is all, *Cool.* Because *what else are you going to do?* Especially when you're six hundred years old, which is what the Bible tells us is Noah's age. The flood comes, raining for forty days, covering mountains and killing everything. *Everything.* All that's left is Noah and what's on the ark. Nothing but water for 150 days. And here's where it gets weird. Suddenly God *remembers* that Noah is down there, floating around with a petting zoo, and God makes a wind blow over the world so that the waters go away. It takes three months for the water to eventually recede, and finally Noah goes, *I'm gonna open this window and see what's what.* A dove appears. God makes a promise that this won't ever happen again and creates a covenant with humanity. The moral of this story is . . . God changes God's mind? God can get fed up? If God tells you to build a boat you should do it? Take your pick. (Also? Noah? Decidedly *not* a cute story for kids, despite all the picture books, nursery wallpaper, and fluffy toys.)

Anyway, know that what we're doing here is good. Normal. And if you ever encounter one of these hot-headed types, just nod and smile, nod and smile. They eventually just go away.

So, the *omnis*.

Of course, as with everything about theology, there are *a lot* more ways of describing the nature of God. These can range from "eternal" to "holy" to "immutable" to "impassible," et cetera. But to *not* turn this into a textbook—and to keep you from deciding this book would make a perfect doorstop—we'll stick with the three *omnis*.

Let's look at each of these individually, in a little more depth.

First, *omnipotence*, or the idea that God is all-powerful. Essentially, this belief means that nothing has power over God. It's pretty easy to find biblical support for this, too. Take this passage from Psalm 135:

For I know that the Lord is great;
our Lord is above all gods.
Whatever the Lord pleases he does,
in heaven and on earth,
in the seas and all deeps. (vv. 5–6)

For most Christians, it's not too challenging to believe
that God is great—above all other gods. Most of us are
taught this as a core fact of monotheism, or the belief that
there is only one God. However, take a moment to consider
this statement from the point of view of people from other
faiths—they might be friends, or even family members.
Saying that our God is above all other gods immediately
creates friction, right? It's important to understand that
we live in a pluralistic society, or a society that is comprised
of people who hold many different beliefs—some religious,
some not. For a long time, Christianity dominated the culture, mostly intentionally. There were a lot of reasons for
this, but one of the big ones was the idea that God is *God*
and we need to make sure *everybody* hears that message.

We don't have the time to dive deep into pluralism, but
know how important it is to have relationships with and
listen to our siblings from other faith traditions. When we
come into interfaith conversations with an openness to
learn new things—not only about their faith but ours as
well—we open ourselves to the opportunity for God to help
us see things in a new way. Or even riskier, the opportunity to have our mind changed!

Okay, back to omnipotence.

The well-known Spider-Man quote applies here: "With great power comes great responsibility." Because the more you unpack the idea of omnipotence, the more it seems to be wrapped in thick, thorny vines.

Does God decide who is born in, say, the United States and therefore has a much greater chance of becoming a Christian instead of the same child being born in, say, Iran?

What about people who decide to leave the faith? Does God know when that person will eventually leave? And if that's the case, does that mean that God can bring that person back into the fold whenever God chooses? A more conservative answer to these questions would be *Well, of course.* God moves the heart of the lost person, *giving* them a "saving" faith.

This is based in two concepts, one that we've already discussed and one that will be new: sovereignty and free will.

Sovereignty, basically, means that God's gonna do what God's gonna do. Again, there's something weirdly comforting about this! And there is definitely support in the Bible for this (just ask Jonah). Many of those stories are wonderful, liberating stories that show us a picture of God that does not care about human-made boundaries—human-designed "answers." (The story of Ruth is another good one!) However, if you're going to talk about sovereignty, you should acknowledge the word games theologians can play. Usually it's something like this: *God does what God desires.* Did you catch that last word? *Desires.* A helpful "out" in some trickier theological situations because, you know, maybe God just wasn't feeling it that day! Maybe God didn't *desire* to help!

Free will is, let's admit it, equally frustrating.

These two ideas are tied together because of one big question: if God can do whatever God wants (or desires) to do, does that mean humans *actually* have free will? Free will is the idea that we can *choose* to act a certain way. What's at stake is whether God controls humans like robots and whether that would be *better* than our current way of living—that is, having the option to create suffering in the world.

The classical view of this means, of course, that we can't influence God's actions. To make things *really* clear, this is both supported and contradicted in scripture! Also, process theologians and those who believe in a missional theology (meaning, a theology that emphasizes working for good in the world) would suggest that we are co-creators or collaborators with God in the world.

Get ready. This is where it gets even more confusing.

Free will essentially means that we can do whatever we want. But it doesn't mean that God isn't trying to influence us through the Holy Spirit. Some theologians would call this *prevenient grace* (which is a grace that moves before we even ask for it). There is something beautiful about this, a God that is constantly seeking us out. Never letting us get too far. A more nefarious version says that God controls everything (remember, omnipotence!) and so God shapes all the different experiences and events in our lives. God also influences our hearts, causing us to be either open-hearted or "hard-hearted" to the choices God puts before us.

So, that's not great. *Bleak* is a word you could use.

And if you're kind of freaking out, know that *you are not alone!* While there are many ways people are introduced to the problem of evil, this is one that will keep you up at night—is it better to be a robot and, perhaps, happy? Or would you rather have free will and be able to freely choose to . . . separate yourself from God?

Bleak.

Of course, it's important to remember that this is only one view of God, and it should be vigorously interrogated—especially if you're sitting there right now thinking, *What in the heck . . . ?* Because there are many ways of discussing how God is present and active in the world.

As always, you must ask yourself: Does this track with the God I know?

The God I've experienced?

Hey, *have* you experienced God before?

This sort of language makes people *extremely* uncomfortable—and for good reason! It has been used in some pretty creepy ways by some pretty creepy Christians, but if you can get past that and really *think* about it for a second—God is *present*.

Like, right here. Right now.

On the positive side, a God who is close—a God who is never going to leave you alone, whether you like it or not—is kind of awesome. There's a strain of theology called *liberation theology* that makes use of this in wonderful ways, saying that God is always close to the so-called margins of society—intimately close with the *least of these*.

A close, present God.

This is our second *omni—omnipresence*.

You might be thinking: "What could be wrong with that?"

(Or you could be totally thinking: "No. I was not even wondering about that. *Later.*" And . . . that's fair.)

The Psalmist really nails this one down for us when they ask, basically, *How in the heck do I get away from you, God? You're in heaven. You're in the middle of the ocean. Like, I just want to get away, and this is really annoying.*

That last part might not be an accurate translation of Psalm 139, but you get the point.

With omnipresence, God is all together (think about the Trinity) at all times. This is pretty cool, especially if you are into science—physics, chemistry, biology, even astronomy. If we believe in an omnipresent God, it means that God is active, involved, and immediate in solar systems that we have not discovered. It means that God is in atoms and subatomic particles. God is involved in gravitation, in the ordering of the planets, in the evolution and development of animal species. And it means that God is present right here, closer than we can imagine.

> The Trinity (c. 0 BCE to c. Forever) is a Christian doctrine that states God is one God while simultaneously existing in the form of three eternal and separate—but ultimately the same—persons, namely the God, Jesus, and the Holy Spirit. It was developed by early Christians to help understand the connection and relationship between Jesus and God in scripture and also in their prior traditions. Confused? You're in good company.

Consider the Bible for a second.

What are some ways that God is present in scripture?

The first one that comes to mind is God appearing to Moses in the form of a burning bush (Exodus 3:1–4:17). Let's never say that God doesn't have a dramatic flair. A burning bush! Just totally on fire and burning while never destroying the bush. It's the sort of thing that makes an impact—just ask Moses.

This is often called *revelation*. Now, don't start worrying about End Times and people disappearing off airplanes—all that business. Revelation, at its most basic theological level, is God presenting a message to someone. Revelation is awesome—and, admittedly, kind of scary. These are the moments we realize that God is close. This is when we are suddenly overtaken by a powerful feeling that we are not alone, that we are cared for in a way that defies our understanding.

Revelation can be a physical thing, as in Moses and the burning bush. But it can also be non-physical, as in when somebody is "filled" with the Holy Spirit.

Okay, let's pause here.

This probably makes you nervous.

But the idea of the Holy Spirit being active in the world—in our lives—is important and not something that progressive-leaning Christians should easily give away to more conservative theological circles.

When the Spirit fills us, it means that we are connected to God. It's as if an antenna has been raised, one that is picking up a frequency that maybe we haven't heard yet.

It's okay to be skeptical. The main point is this: God can be physically present through revelation, or it can be a non-physical manifestation. But in both situations, God is *always present even if we don't realize it.*

We intentionally seek out God's presence in a number of ways. The most notable one for most Christians is worship, but we can't say that God only shows up at church!

Have you ever been snowboarding or reading and felt closer to God?

Or had a song come on the radio, and it just feels *true,* as if it's being sung to you?

This is what people mean when they say they "find God in nature" or call themselves "spiritual but not religious." It's based in the idea that God is out there—we just need to notice. God is everywhere.

Next up—and this one makes a lot of people cranky—is *omniscient*, or a God who is all-knowing. Or to put it a different way, there is nothing new to God. There are no surprises. God can see throughout all of history and into the future. Again, the Bible—this time from the Letter of Paul to the Romans—gives us a starting point:

For those whom he foreknew he also predestined to be conformed to the image of his Son, in order that he might be the firstborn within a large family. (8:29)

Okay, this is a bit of a cheat.

This is what you might call a *proof text*, or a verse from the Bible that is separated from its original context to make a point . . . or win an argument. Either way, proof texting is almost always considered a *faux pas* in theology circles, because it's important to consider the context, the audience and intent, of a passage.

Still. There's a *glaring* word in that passage that likely makes you itch.

Take a second. See if you can figure it out.

waiting

waiting

waiting

Okay—it's another one of those words that's been co-opted by gross people with gross theology. But let's just say it out loud, all together now.

Predestined.

Predestination is a theological term that either makes sense or it doesn't. There aren't many people who find themselves in the middle of this doctrine. And it's a doctrine that is *very* connected to an idea of God being omniscient. All-knowing. Predestination means that *all events* in history have been willed by God. Our friend *Free Will* is back again! Predestination is often used as an answer to the "paradox of free will" or the idea that God being omniscient and humans having free will are incompatible ideas. However, this gets itchy for people when it comes to salvation. Does God choose who is "saved" and who is not and there's nothing we can do about it?

Itchy.

Still, there are likely parts of this that . . . also kind of make sense, right?

How could God *not* know everything?

It's . . . God.

Think about the scene with Jesus and the disciples on a boat being tossed around by tall waves (Luke 8:22–25). The disciples are worried—as they should be! Because Jesus is, you know, sound asleep. Totally unconcerned. When they finally wake him up, he's like, "What, this?" And with the wave of a hand—a Jesus Jedi mind trick, so to speak—suddenly the storm has passed.

Hear this: it is not bad to trust God. It is not bad to find yourself in the middle of the storm and to call out to God for help. When people say, "God has a plan," they're trying to cut through the anxiety that comes with living through tragedies, big and small.

But—tell me if you've heard this one before—there are some things that should make you pause.

When somebody speaks about God's plan, they're suggesting that God has determined—before creation—every single moment of history, of your lives. The big things, the small things. All of it. The rub comes during times of tragedy. It requires us to ask: where was God during the atrocity of the Holocaust? What about war? Acts of terrorism? Global poverty, the environmental crisis, COVID-19, cancer—the list is nearly endless.

How do we account for God's seeming inaction in history, if God is indeed all-knowing? (Not to mention present and powerful!)

Now, there are a few ways people *solve* this problem.

First, the get-out-of-jail-free card for this is to say, "Of course God didn't know everything that was going to happen—*Free Will!*—but God knows *the end* of the plan and how that will work out."

Well, fair.

You can go pretty far down the road with that argument.

But ultimately, you still arrive at the big question—*why?*

On the other hand, process theology (which we should admit is still controversial; lots of people get *very* upset if you suggest that God might not know everything that's going to happen) flips the idea of the omniscient God on its head. In process theology, God is not all-knowing. Or to put a finer point on it: God does not know the future. There are many reasons for this, but mostly it's centered around the fact that God can't know something that isn't a reality. So, once something "is" (this is getting heady, but stick with it for one more second), then God can know it. From there, God allows humans to make a series of choices based on the current reality.

This is radical stuff.

It suggests that God is not fixed. It suggests that God can change based on our actions. It means that God can turn any situation into a new situation, one that we might not expect—to produce fruit that we might not ever be able to see.

For some, this is a comfort.

For others, this is heresy.

Again, not many people land in the middle!

At the crux is the power of God, which is how we will end this portion of our discussion. If you believe in the *omnis,* you can rest firmly in the grip of a God who is uniquely and unilaterally powerful. The concern with process theology is that it weakens God—how can we ever find comfort in a God who can't know what's going to happen? Who, for lack of a better term, is simply along for the ride?

The good (and maybe bad!) news is: only you can answer this for yourself.

When it comes to the *omnis*—to all of theology!—*you* get to decide what stays in your theodicy. These do not have to stand or fall together. There might be seasons in your life where one makes sense and others do not. And then later, you might find yourself growing in a new direction.

Hear this again: *You get to decide.*

That's the beauty—and the power—of the doing theology. Of being a theologian.

If you're feeling a little squishy on this, that's natural. Perhaps you're wondering how you might find some actual evidence to back up your evolving beliefs.

For Christians, the first place to look is the Bible.

6

What Does the Bible Say?

The Bible is important.

Look, you knew you were coming to this book to get the *real deal* insights, right? So, there you go. Money in your pocket. Let your priest or pastor know that you learned something.

The Bible is important.

This might seem obvious and, granted, something that doesn't need to be articulated. However, when we are trying to figure out the character or nature of God, it's natural to turn to the collection of writings from two different faith traditions for some insights.

To that end, let's clear something up quickly. There are not two Gods in the Bible. There isn't an "Old Testament God" and a different "New Testament God." This notion is based on the perceived difference of the wrath of God and the love of God—and too often, becomes the basis for anti-Semitism and hate. This is most notably connected to Marcion, and it kicked off centuries of arguments. However, despite being considered outside the bounds of orthodox Christianity, Marcionism still persists . . . even if people have no idea who Marcion is!

> **Marcion of Sinope** (c. 85 CE to c. 160 CE) was an early Christian theologian and, later in life, was 100 percent deemed a heretic by many of the early church fathers. While he's known for his Old Testament/New Testament views of God, he was also the first person to publish a collection of Christian documents. And! The New Testament we have now came together a lot faster because people were like, *Oh we aren't about to let this guy have the final word.*

Many modern theologians are uncomfortable with the wrath of God. Which makes sense! How do we square *that* with a loving God? Theologians like James Cone would say that God reveals God's self as love and eternal faithfulness throughout scripture. Wrath, however, should be seen as God's *righteousness*—or God's inability to see injustice in the world and not respond. It means that God takes a side against injustice.

James Cone (1938 to 2018) was a theologian known for connecting Black Power ideology with Christian theology, saying that white supremacy had denied Black people the chance to be human and was the actual gospel of the United States. In Cone's theology, Jesus came to liberate the oppressed—which was the same as Black Power. Cone was radical and remains influential in the church.

A God that is separated from wrath does not plan on liberating or saving anyone. Cone says, "A God minus wrath seems to be a God who is basically not against anything. All we have to do is behave nicely, and everything will work out all right."

We've beaten that dead horse enough.

If you feel the urge to think about a *Before Jesus* God and an *After Jesus* God . . . take a breath. Do some yoga. Be on the right side of theology!

All kidding aside, it's important to recognize and affirm that the God of the Old Testament is the same as the God of the New Testament.

Whew. Let's take a breath.

Are you good?

You look good.

What *does* the Bible say about God?

Well, *a lot.* So, we'll try to narrow it down and focus on some of the overarching themes that are applied to God throughout both the Hebrew Bible and the Christian Scriptures.

First, God is *present.*

For a second, ignore the omnipresent part of the last chapter. Because the idea that God is *present*—to us, among us, with us, for us—is completely bananas.

Like, a truck full of bananas being dumped on your front lawn, *bananas.*

God's presence gives us rest, it travels with us throughout our lives. It draws near to us. God's presence will purify your heart, cleanse your hands. It's God saying, "I have made promises to you, and I'm not going anywhere until those promises are fulfilled." It promises that God will be with us, always—to the end of time.

This, too, is radical stuff.

And it's all in the Bible.

Again and again God reminds us that everything is going to change—it's inevitable, a foregone conclusion. The world we see right now does not have the final answer because God is disrupting all things that bring injustice, inequality.

The presence of God is *radical* because it ultimately leads us to *redemption* and *deliverance.*

You look uncomfortable.

"Redemption" and "deliverance." That's what did it, right?

Much like *revelation*, redemption and deliverance have become co-opted by religious people who are more interested in excluding people rather than including them. It's ironic because redemption is based in the idea that there is no mess you can make, no sin you can commit, *nothing you can do*, that will separate you from God.

Redemption is a big deal.

It tells us that God can look at our biggest disasters and say, "Yep, I got that. Oh, and that one too. And that huge pile you tried to hide behind the door? Yep. I got it."

God redeems all things.

God redeems *all things*.

The prophet Isaiah puts it this way:

> *Do not fear, for I have redeemed you;*
> *I have called you by name, you are mine.*
>   (Isaiah 43:1b)

I have called you by name.

You are mine.

God knows us by name. God claims us as God's own. This is likely something you've heard in Sunday school or during worship. But take a moment to really think about the idea that God knows you by name—and not only knows you but calls for you to come closer. To set aside all the messiness of your life, all the things that are embarrassing or painful. God says: Don't worry about that. Just come to me.

God is a redeemer.

And God delivers, too.

You can think about this in two ways.

First—and perhaps most simply—God can be trusted. Even in the most unbelievable situations, the God of the Bible stands true to God's word. Now, be warned—this isn't always great! You could be a really old woman and suddenly you've got a crying baby on your hip. Or you could be just a run-of–the-mill shepherd and suddenly, like, you're king.

> Sarah was Abraham's wife and even though she was *really* old God was like, "You're about to have some babies. Mother of *nations!*" (Genesis 17:16). David was a shepherd—had a disagreement with a guy named Goliath you may have heard about—and ultimately ended up king (1 and 2 Samuel). God can use anyone—and often the people we least expect.

The joke goes: if you want to hear divine laughter, tell God your plans.

If God says something is going to happen in the Bible, it happens.

However, this is a slightly limited view of deliverance. From a theological standpoint, *deliverance* means that God is not unmoved by the actions of the world. The biggest example is the story told in the book of Exodus. Basically, the Israelites are slaves in Egypt. God calls Moses to confront Pharaoh, who has decided that he's on the same level as God.

Quick note here: this never turns out well.

Anyway, Pharaoh and the Egyptians suffer through a number of pretty horrendous plagues (including the death [murder?] of all the firstborn sons of Egypt, which logically would be mostly people who were not involved in this power struggle between God and Pharaoh). Finally, after needless suffering and carnage, Pharaoh agrees to let the Israelites go—to be free.

God leads them through the desert, using a pillar of clouds during the day and a pillar of fire at night. Pharaoh, in perhaps not the smartest move, decides that he isn't going to keep his end of the bargain and sends soldiers to stop the Israelites.

Maybe you saw the movie? If not, read about it in Exodus 14.

God separates the water of the Red Sea, allowing the Israelites to pass through to safety. When the Egyptian chariots try to cross . . .

Well, let's just say this is a good story in terms of discussing theodicy.

No, the Egyptians were far from blameless. But we're talking about the death of countless men—on top of the people who had already perished during the plagues—and while this is certainly a story of deliverance, shouldn't we be asking an even bigger question?

As always: *"Why?"*

On the one hand, many people have constructed liberation theologies—theologies meant to free oppressed or marginalized people—from this story. Again, this is a story of God hearing the cries of God's people and saying, "I will help." On the other hand, this is a story of God murdering people . . . and it's not the only one in scripture!

It's important to remember the word *myth* here.

Ask yourself what's the *point* of the story—think about the intended audience of the story. This was a story told to help people remember that God shows up—God delivers God's people when they are in need. And it's a story that is told today during the Jewish holiday of Passover.

It's an important story for both Jews and Christians because it tells us something about God's character.

This is a good time to introduce the concept of *both/and*.

When somebody says "both/and" it likely means that the story or concept—such as this one—being discussed can be read in various ways. In the Exodus story, we can be reminded of the power of God, while also remembering the importance of not becoming so blinded by *our* stories that we forget to look for how those stories might impact other people.

So, what's the takeaway?

God is our advocate, God is present, even in situations that seem hopeless. Or to quote Monica Coleman, God can make a way out of no way.

Let's end on a piece of theology you likely already know.

God is love.

God is love!

By itself, it can be a powerful message, a reminder that God's love is something we can't fully comprehend. It expands past any boundaries we try to set up for it, growing and growing until it has encompassed every single person who has been told they're not worthy, every person who has rejected or cursed it, every single person, no matter what.

God is love.

That might be the single most powerful theological sentence you can say. It's both a declaration and an accountability check. When somebody makes a theological claim, one of the first things you can do to test it is to ask whether a good and loving God would endorse the statement.

It's also the attribute that gets people the most frustrated in the Bible stories. Because there are several stories that seemingly contradict what we've just learned about God's character. In the book of Jeremiah (31:15), Rachel, the matriarch of three of the tribes of Israel, is shown weeping and inconsolable over the loss of her children, who have been taken into captivity. The point is to show us a character to help us identify with the trauma caused by exile—a story about *real* suffering even when the hope of God is known, believed, and experienced. Rachel's is a story short on hope, or at least *easy* hope. While there is definitely a theological claim to be made that God is present even in the tragedy of her loss—remember that?—even in the midst of such deep suffering, it can be a hollow and tone-deaf response in the face of such mourning. With Rachel, we see the importance of naming the stuff that breaks us—the stuff that makes it seem impossible to find healing in. We see that, sometimes, our circumstances can be overwhelming.

On that note, it's time.

Perhaps the most well-known example of a "WTH, God?" moment comes in the book of Job (which, fun fact, is mostly likely the oldest book in the Bible).

Ironically, the Job narrative is meant to address the problem of theodicy.

Job is wealthy, a man who loves God. He lives a comfortable, blessed life—shared by his large family.

And this is where it gets kind of twisted.

God is just hanging around in heaven, presumably, and he's like, "Hey, Satan, what do you think about old Job? That guy would *never* curse me. Never turn his back on me. Job is my first-round draft pick when it comes to this whole faith thing!"

Let's pause for a second.

Why in the heck is "the satan" just hanging around with God?

And—perhaps a broader point—why *is* Satan? Like, c'mon God. You couldn't make things a little easier for people. You couldn't see *that* turning bad?

(Slight aside: You don't have to believe in the satan or the devil or Lucifer—none of it. Satan means, simply, "the adversary.")

Anyway.

Satan is like, "The only reason that dude is holy and good is because you literally gave him *everything*. If you take that stuff away, he's gonna curse your name immediately. Believe that."

Now, this is important. God does not take anything away. Satan is granted permission to take away Job's wealth, kill his children and servants. He lets Satan go *hard*.

So, Satan does his worst, and Job is like, "Nope. Not gonna do it. God gives, God takes away. Not today, Satan!"

So, Satan ups his game. Gives him boils, which . . . if you're brave, just look it up. It gets so bad that eventually Job is sitting in ashes and his wife—a realist, frankly—says, "Just curse God and die!"

Not exactly what you'd expect from the person who promised to be with you "for better or worse."

Anyway, old Job isn't having it. He says, "Hey, if we're going to receive good from God, we're also going to get some evil in there too."

Warning bells. Red flags. You see them, right?

Well, it gets better. Job has these three friends who show up just after all of this has gone down. Instead of helping Job, these jokers start wondering aloud if he was going through all these troubles because he sinned—and then they're like, "Hey maybe you *deserve* it."

Another quick aside: If your friends are going through literally the worst moment of their lives, this is *not the moment to become a theologian.* Or at least, you should learn to keep that mess to yourself until you've asked the only question that needs to be asked: "How can I help?" Or simply: "I'm here for you."

But no. Job needs friends and he gets a bunch of theologians instead, calling them "miserable comforters," which, given everything, is both accurate and pretty hilarious.

This is where it gets good.

Because Job is officially over it.

Job had some of the same questions you do.

Job wants to know why a just God would treat him so badly—why he would be treated with such disregard.

It's a radical, radical statement and sentiment, perhaps the most radical in the entire Bible. From there, Job goes off. He yells at God for the harsh treatment. He is angry. And he quickly moves on from *his* problems to all the problems that God seems to allow in the world. He calls out God for not helping the helpless, the needy.

Maybe this is a good theodicy after all.

What comes from God is either deeply comforting . . . or not.

God speaks to Job from a whirlwind, which is *definitely* a power move. And God does not defend Job's treatment, refusing to be brought into the realm of justice as humans see it. Instead, God goes kind of parental on Job—"Oh, you think you're a grown man? Well, where were you when I was *literally* putting together the earth? Yeah, the *earth.*"

This continues back and forth for a little bit, before Job finally concedes and is like, "I didn't know you were going to bring up all *that*."

In the end, Job is restored to health and receives both his riches and a (new) family back, living a long life.

Job is traditionally seen as an investigation (interrogation?) of divine justice, of the problem of theodicy. Before this story, the idea was simple: God punishes bad people and rewards good people. It's the reason Job's friends respond the way they do—this was baked into the way their culture thought about God.

But are the answers we receive from this story helpful?

Many, many people have said no.

Perhaps you're among them.

Again, it's important to remember context—to remember *why* people were telling this story. It's like the reason you're reading this book, perhaps. You had a question and wanted an answer. Similarly, the writers of Job were trying to explain a problem that affected every single aspect of their lives.

How could they *know* that God would protect them?

How could they know and *trust* God?

No matter how you slice it, though, it's an unsatisfactory answer to the question of why bad things happen—why God allows it.

And maybe that's the point.

Maybe we're asked to encounter the story of Job, not looking for answers but finding a place of commiseration, a shared connection with other people who have suffered, who have blamed God for that suffering—people who love God and scream out in those dark nights, "God, why?!"

It's an honest and pure question, perhaps the most honest question that can be asked by a theologian—by a person such as yourself.

So, what do we do with all of . . . this?

What can we say about God?

The start of that answer might be in the other stories of the Bible. The stories that show us a God of love, a God of redemption. A God who is always present, no matter what, always working to deliver us from the brokenness and pain of this world.

No Clever Title: The Chapter about Suffering

Much of the conversation surrounding theodicy assumes that sin is the primary reason for the existence of evil. This, of course, can be argued in good and not-so-good ways. On the one hand, yes—we can certainly name various *sins*.

Racism.

Climate change.

Poverty

War.

Police violence.

We could go on and on.

However, a theodicy that is primarily based in *sin* also concedes that something has gone wrong, or someone (some*thing*) is to blame. Usually, that means either us or God. And its humans who are going to lose out in that hypothetical scenario—especially in the church.

We have a question of intent or impact.

Let's talk that out a bit.

Do you believe God intentionally creates evil in the world as a way for us to learn lessons, grow, or somehow see life in a new and different way?

If so, that's *intent*.

It means that evil—the problem of pain and suffering—is intentionally a feature of the system and not a mistake. If we go too far down this road, we'll need to deal with the question we've been circling together for much of this conversation—can God be considered *good* in this scenario? Or is God somehow malevolent? Sadistic?

Another way to look at it would be to think of evil as an impact, or an effect. And not just any old effect but an *outrageous* effect—something that is so offensive to some innate part of our minds, bodies, and souls that it creates existential (as in, the sort you can't stop thinking about) crises.

Sound familiar?

These are the big questions, ones that don't have nice, neat answers. They are outrageous questions to a problem that should enrage us. *We should not accept or normalize the suffering of people.* When we pass an unhoused person, we should ask *why*. We should investigate the systems, the status quo, that allow for people to go without basic human needs. When we hear about a person being evicted from their home during a pandemic, *we should act to stop the injustice.*

What if the problem of evil—theodicy—is the result of an outrageous effect and not some sort of divine game?

If that's the case, then we have to shift our ideas about theodicy from a focus on sin to a focus on suffering.

Here's a fancy theologian name you can drop the next time you're in a heady theological conversation: Wendy Farley.

> **Wendy Farley** (b. 1958) is a theologian who is known for reenvisioning major theological topics (such as . . . theodicy!) while focusing on marginalized people and concerns. Her first book, *Tragic Vision and Divine Compassion*, is a major influence on the second half of *this* book.

Wendy Farley asks this exact question—what if the problem of evil is actually about suffering? What if there is suffering out there that simply can't be explained—*radical suffering* that dehumanizes and destroys *all* of us simply by its mere existence?

If you look back at the (Mostly) Dead Theologians Answer Club, you're going to find a lot of so-called *classical* theologians who are hyper-focused on sin, on what humans did to cause the pain and suffering we all endure. This creates a sort of "hero" and "villain" setup, where there are good ways to act and bad ways to act and, depending on your theology, you can either try *really* hard and avoid sin or pray that God forgives you.

But if we follow Farley and consider theodicy as an effect of suffering—radical suffering that extends across all of humanity, trapping us in a spiderweb of impossible choices—it can no longer be a neat, easy fight of good vs. evil.

Let's go back to sin for a moment.

Sin is serious.

This is true in the Bible, both Old and New Testaments, and as we discussed previously, it should be serious for us as well.

Sin is separation from God.

And even though we can't *really* be separated from God . . .

We still try our best.

Heck, that gray area might be a good description of sin—our attempts to hide in the Garden, despite God's attempts to find us.

However, sin as a *personal* problem versus sin as a *corporate* or *communal* thing that affects all of us is an important distinction. This is the spiderweb, the network of decisions that are made on our behalf—decisions we make without ever seeing the consequences, without realizing that our actions have created suffering.

You go to the store and buy a t-shirt.

Seems basic, right?

But that t-shirt was made in a developing company, where the employees are paid pennies a day. And say you know this, but you are a working mother with three kids and the kids need clothes for school. This is the only shirt you can afford.

What do you do?

Are you committing a sin?

Wendy Farley tells us that sin is both a theological and an ethical category. That means that sin just isn't something we struggle with personally—it isn't saying a cuss word or rooting for the New York Yankees.

I mean, it *can* be those things, but it isn't limited to our personal actions.

Instead, when Wendy Farley says sin is also an ethical category, it means that we must see sin as something that manifests in the world as cruelty, injustice—something that hurts all of us, even if we can't see it.

So, to reframe a discussion about the problem of evil around suffering means that we turn our questions—and more importantly, our actions—away from the *hows* and *whys* that surround God and point them at the real-world causes and effects of sin and suffering.

This got deep quick.

Take a breath.

Anybody know a good joke?

Okay, here's one:

How do pirates know that they are pirates?

They think, therefore they *ARRR!*

Speaking of suffering . . .

Ahem.

Anyway, what happens when we frame the question of evil around suffering instead of sin?

To answer this question, I think we need to invite Wendy Farley to . . .

● ● ●

The (Fully Alive) Theologians Club

(An empty room with a comfortable chair at the center. A single spotlight falls on it, covering Wendy Farley in a soft, glowing light.)

MODERATOR

Well, isn't this a surprise! An actual living theologian here with us.

WENDY FARLEY

Yes, well, I'm pretty sure some of the other theologians were alive—shout-out to the Womanists.

MODERATOR

Fair enough! Dr. Farley, we are here to talk about suffering! Are you ready?!

FARLEY

You seem awfully chipper about this, but okay . . .

MODERATOR

I can't help it! Theology really gets my blood pumping!

(An awkward silence as the two stare at each other.)

MODERATOR

Okay, well—why should we think about theodicy in terms of suffering?

FARLEY

Well, when we describe it in terms of suffering, we allow ourselves to retain "the sharp edge of anger" at the unfairness and destructiveness we see in the world. When we do this, we admit that we can't stay separated from the suffering—we have to admit that we are angry! So, we are no longer trying to explain it and definitely not trying to justify it.

MODERATOR

Ah, I understand. So, we aren't allowed to play the theological game of pretending that we are somehow an objective observer . . .

FARLEY

Yes, exactly. But it's not just anger. We also feel the deep sorrow of knowing that suffering exists. And that leads us to be *changed* by the suffering we see.

MODERATOR

Is this different than saying that suffering changes us—helps us to grow or learn things?

FARLEY

Not really. Not in the classical sense that there's a *reason* for suffering. I would say that seeing and experiencing suffering shocks us out of the belief that what's happening all around us—the severe pain and suffering we see in the world—is *not normal*. It desensitizes us.

MODERATOR
Right. And this is what you call *radical suffering*.

FARLEY
Yes! Some kinds of suffering are irredeemable. You cannot justify it. And this is the problem with a lot of those (Mostly) Dead Theologians' theodicies. They want to justify it and . . . you can't. Not without some serious repercussions.

MODERATOR
This is where you usually talk about tragedy.

FARLEY
Wow, you're good at this. Well done.

MODERATOR
Thank you.

FARLEY
Yes, well, I like to think about theodicy as a tragedy, instead of the "fall of humanity." The Fall, again, justifies suffering—it tells us that a myth is the reason that people hurt, that they suffer. Yes, it tells us that we'll get relief eventually, in heaven, but doesn't it make better sense for us to work to relieve suffering right now? To expect things to be addressed right now, in the real world?

MODERATOR

I think this might help us understand the story of Job a little better. One of the things that makes it difficult is . . . Job doesn't deserve this.

FARLEY

Exactly! It's tragic to see a good person suffer. It cannot be understood as deserved in any way. And if we can't think about it being deserved for *them*, perhaps that means it's not deserved for anybody—perhaps it gives us a new way to think through some of these problems. Tragedy helps us name suffering as a starting point and it gives us permission to be really angry!

MODERATOR

This has been very helpful, Dr. Farley. Thank you for your time.

FARLEY

You're most welcome. I have no idea how I got here, but I'm glad it helped.

*(Dr. Farley stands up, ready to leave
when she stops abruptly.)*

FARLEY

Oh! I almost forgot. Once you realize that none of this is justified, it means that you must defiantly resist suffering in all ways. It means the horror of suffering will provoke you to resist any principalities, any powers, that might create this suffering.

MODERATOR
We're going to be talking about that in our next chapter!

FARLEY
Well, then. Happy disrupting, everybody!

• • •

This is like having a rug pulled out from under your feet.

It's also guilty, somewhat, of playing the sort of games theologians *love* to play—namely, to talk about a problem and spin everything in circles until the whole world is so dizzy that the answer is almost confusing as the original question.

But there's a concrete step buried in Wendy Farley's theodicy.

It's a question we can ask ourselves, one that doesn't answer our questions about why evil exists, naturally. But perhaps it gives us a different starting point—one that helps us refocus our questions, while also relieving some of that existential stress, which is just a bonus.

How do we create suffering?

Let's pause for a second and say that this is not meant to be another question that keeps you up at night. This is not a "beat yourself up" question. Instead, think of it as a different way of looking at the problem of evil. A way to ask how suffering is a result of material (not *divine*) actions that happen in the world.

Now, this doesn't let God off the hook!

It doesn't mean our questions are suddenly not valid.

Because even if we spend the rest of our lives working for justice, it's not simply a matter of doing more work—of being *better*. Ultimately, the work of redeeming and restoring the world falls on God. And good thing! But . . .

We—every single one of us—are called as collaborators, co-conspirators in this work. We're obligated to this work. And asking how we might be able to lessen the suffering of the world, even in the smallest of ways, is a good place to start.

So, you might be thinking—great! How do we fight against this? How do we get started?

Turn the page.

Resistance Isn't Futile

This is the chapter you've been waiting for.

Because this is the chapter where we will reveal . . .

The answer.

That's right! A foolproof, honest-to-God *answer* to the problem of evil!

Are you unsure?

If so, well done. That's what the professionals call a *hermeneutic of suspicion* and what your ornery uncle who lives off the grid up in Alaska might call a *B.S. detector.*

Either way, the instinct is correct. The *answer,* much like the rest of this book, is more of a tool than a bandage that you can wrap all your questions around and come back a few weeks later to find them completely healed.

So, it's not that kind of answer. But if you've made it this far, you might be wondering—what the heck is the point? This whole book has been a complete downer, so thanks for that! What's next? Are you going to introduce a dog character that gets lost and ends up in the city pound? *Awesome.*

Well, no.

But perhaps this chapter will bring about something different, a reminder that you are not powerless when it comes to the evil and suffering in the world.

Or, as the chapter title says, it's a reminder that resistance is *not* futile.

Resistance to suffering—the idea that it is normal—is not futile.

This is the Good News.

This is the story of our faith.

We are not meant to live this way, broken and suffering. And if we believe that—even if we don't believe it but want it to be true—then it means there is the smallest sliver of an opportunity. A chance to wiggle a fingernail into that crack, to widen it just a bit. To work it back and forth until it's just a little bigger—so we can see the possibility of a different world just a little better. And then maybe others see it too and they start to work to widen the crack.

Resistance is not futile.

We won't bring Wendy Farley back to the (Fully Alive) Theologians Club, but her response to this question is a word you've probably heard before.

Compassion.

Nothing fancy about that word. It isn't Latin; it won't make your priest or pastor raise an eyebrow and wonder what they're teaching kids in theology books these days. It's not that kind of word. But make no mistake, it might be the most important word in this book.

When we recognize suffering, when we acknowledge the people who are suffering, we engage in compassion. And this sort of compassion flies in the face of systems that expect people to turn a blind eye to the problems of the world—the big things that get turned into inevitabilities. Compassion is imagination. It's the inquisitive kid at the back of the classroom who won't stop raising their hand, questioning the teacher. Compassion cuts through all the theological crap and reminds all of us that on the other side of these conversations are real people who need help.

You might be thinking, *Hold up.* Isn't compassion, like, me just being all up in my feelings?

Well, yeah. It can be.

But in this case, compassion is more than just *feeling* something. Farley would say that compassion is more than just an emotion but instead is a powerful tool that can be used to confront injustice. We're able to do this because—as we learned before—when we see suffering, we realize that it is real. We can *understand* and *empathize with* the suffering of other people—even if we don't know the specifics of their suffering.

So you don't have to experience being unhoused to have compassion.

You don't have to struggle with food insecurity to have compassion.

You don't have to know somebody on death row to have compassion.

Because you've suffered, you are connected with that person on the street, the struggling parent at the grocery store. The death row inmate.

Compassion is resistance.

Compassion calls for a response and requires action.

Compassion *is* an answer.

Okay, who are the skeptics in the room?

If you aren't sure if you're a skeptic, here's a quick quiz for you.

As you were reading this were you secretly thinking, "Okay, but . . ."?

Congrats! You are a skeptic! And that's not a bad thing. In fact, skeptics are often close to prophets (hopefully without the whole "I'm probably gonna get some stones thrown in my direction for delivering this message . . ." thing) in that they are willing to ask difficult questions. They need to *see* the answer more clearly before they sign up.

Skeptics can be annoying if you're trying to get a group of people to try out a new pizza place, but when it comes to theology, they are critically important.

When Wendy Farley talks about compassion, she's acknowledging that the skeptics in the room have a point. There is a disbelief that compassion can be powerful—that it can be the answer to this question. She calls it the "folly of compassion" because the powers that are at work to create and sustain evil in the world will not see compassion as a threat.

Not all power is meant to coerce, Farley says. Instead, compassion gives power to *other people*. It says, "You're hurting, and I see that. I can help. I will respond. I will not be desensitized to the pain in the world. I am going to show up."

And that, friends, is radical stuff. It is subversive to care about other people, especially in a world that tells you that you must always be looking for ways to win. A world that prioritizes competition and individuality. A world that sees asking for help as a weakness—better to suffer in silence!

No.

Louder for the people in the back: *No.*

We are not meant to live as individuals. That doesn't mean you can't decide to dye your hair pink or to wear bow ties because, frankly, they suit you *quite well*. That's all fine and good—you wear those Crocs with socks. More power to you.

That's not what this is about.

We are not meant to suffer alone. We are meant to live in community—in communion with one another. We are called, by God, to create a beloved community where equality and justice are the norms.

"Beloved Community," popularized by Dr. Martin Luther King Jr., is a society based on justice, equality, and love for one another. Christians of many denominations work to foster Beloved Community in the world, so that we can all grow as reconcilers, justice-seekers, and healers in the name of God. (However, this is aspirational language—not something that has already been realized! It's in process!)

And this starts with something as simple as compassion. Before we move on, let's go back to the *omnis* for a second.

Oh Lord, help us now in our time of trial . . .

No, no—it's going to be okay. You're going to like this.

looks sideways

Really, you will.

Remember Jürgen Moltmann? Old Jürgen (another fun word to say, right? *Jürgen*) developed a theory of the "cruci-fied God," which, basically, says that God knows all of our pain and suffering—and not only that, God is *with us* in our pain and suffering.

You might be thinking, "Cool story, bro."

But consider how this works with an omniscient God. God *literally* knows all suffering. God literally *experiences* all suffering. And if that is true—if we can acknowledge that God experiences suffering and, therefore, must have a similar response to suffering . . .

Wait for it . . .

Wait for it . . .

Kind of sounds like an answer.

A small answer, for sure, and not an all-encompassing answer. But if how we relate to one another is a glimpse of the attributes of God, then perhaps it's a peek behind the theological curtain for us as well.

Perhaps we are slowly unworking the evil and suffering that (Maybe? Maybe not?) started at the Fall. Now, again, you don't have to believe in the Fall to appreciate the message behind this.

We are moving forward.

Things are getting better.

And that starts with compassion.

9

Another Necessary Interlude!

It's time for Another Necessary Interlude!

Friends, you certainly deserve this one.

Let's check in.

How are you doing? What are you feeling? Do you still want to throw this book against the wall, or perhaps *at* the person who put it in your hands?

While violence is never the answer, let's honor whatever feelings you might be feeling. Let's accept them without judgment, without anxiety. Let's say, *"Okay—this is where I am right now."*

Perhaps you're feeling excited, energized.

Or maybe you're hesitating.

You might be more confused than ever.

And every single one of these is valid, real, and true. Which might *not* be helpful! But what you're undertaking in this book is risky. It requires legit courage. You are wading into the deep end of the pool, and people are yelling "Hey! Do you want this unicorn floatie?" And you give them a steely-eyed stare, the kind you see in movies, and shake your head solemnly. Maybe you even give them an action movie quote. Something like, "Where I'm going, I have to go alone."

Totally metal.

The point is: Whatever you're feeling is right. And if you need some time to process those feelings, take it.

That might mean playing a video game.

Or watching some anime.

Hey, it looks like your dog might want to go on a walk, and I can tell that he is a *very good boy*.

Decompress. Take a breath. And come back when you're ready.

. . .

. . .

. . .

But when you come back, think about the power of compassion. Not only compassion for other people but compassion for yourself.

Especially as we move forward into some *real-life* examples—many of which are going to frustrate you because the answer is *I don't know*.

We don't know!

Don't let it stress you out. If you really need a break, just skip through the real-life stuff—some of it might be more *real-life* than you can handle right now—and flip to the next chapter. Come back later. Maybe with a snack.

A snack sounds like a really good idea right now.

You get a snack and when you come back, we'll end with a quote.

You are walking to the kitchen.

You are opening the refrigerator.

*You are totally getting a healthy snack and *not* some of that ice cream that you aren't supposed to touch before dinner but, hey, you deserve it right now because this whole *reading a book about theodicy* thing has been a bit much so we're not going to say a word.*

Hey, you're back!

Let's end with a quote—well, it's not *exactly* a quote so let's call it a prayer.

It's by way of another theologian named Paul Tillich, adapted from a sermon he wrote called "You Are Accepted."

Paul Tillich (1886 to 1965) is a theologian best known for his books *The Courage to Be* and *Dynamics of Faith*, both of which were for non-academic, popular audiences. He is known for many things, and one of them is that he believed God could only be spoken about in symbolic language.

Ready?

• • •

You are accepted.

You are accepted by something so great.

You might not know what that means, but
that's okay.
You might not be ready to ask why—and that's
okay
Because one day, you'll be ready.
One day, the skies will part, and you'll remem-
ber these words.
You are accepted.
Amen.

• • •

10

Big Hairy Questions and Other Tedious Things

Hopefully things are a little clearer right now. But clarity doesn't mean not having questions. It doesn't mean those answers won't eventually stretch out a bit—won't fit the same way they do now.

Cheery, right?

Still, those answers you've fought hard to cobble together as you've read this book? Totally valid. Sit with them. Find peace in them. And interrogate them whenever you can.

As we live, we experience new things. Some of these experiences will be deeply good, moments that are burned into our very being. Some of them will be difficult. Some may even define you in ways you can't possibly comprehend right now. These are the moments when it is critical to be able to think theologically—to construct your conceptions about God with a little flexibility. A chance to receive new information.

Don't let this bum you out. But as long as you're building a theodicy, make sure it isn't something you'll outgrow your first year of college.

So, let's play.

Think of some Big Questions, things you might worry about or maybe have even experienced yourself.

And hear this part again: we're going to *play*.

That means you can take some chances.

You can laugh.

You can take a moment and—as serious as some of these topics are—give yourself a chance to be wrong. To be unsure about where you will land. Don't mistake *play* with a lack of seriousness. Play is important and, frankly, something many of us give up way too early in our lives.

Being able to play allows for creativity, for imagination. It allows us to see different possibilities without the burden of being *right* or *wrong*.

So, let's give it a shot. Let's see where we end up.

● ● ●

Hitler

Might as well start off with a bang, right?

First, let's get this out of the way: there's nothing playful or funny about Hitler or about the genocide he engineered. The Holocaust remains perhaps the biggest theological (and ethical) obstacle we must contend with as people of faith.

There is no way to justify it.

There is no way to understand it.

This was and continues to be a tragedy.

As a result, whenever people are trying to figure out a theological problem—especially if they haven't been introduced to theology in a significant way—we will eventually end up with what can very quickly become a conversation killer.

What about Hitler?

Now, this question usually comes at a point when you're discussing a variety of topics:

1. Salvation (or *eschatology*, which is another fancy word you can use to impress your friends—you're welcome).
2. Our responsibilities toward other people.
3. The problem of evil.

Because, let's face it, Hitler was a monster—the epitome of evil. It's no wonder he's the go-to example, the example that seeks to, if we're being honest, show whether your theology is full of crap or not.

Here's what's at stake: if God is willing to forgive Hitler for what he did to millions of Jews during the Holocaust, what does that say about God?

And if God *does* punish Hitler . . . where do we draw the line when it comes to heaven and hell? Is hell only for people who are *really* bad? And if that's the case, what does *really* bad mean? (Whether there's a heaven and a hell, and where those ideas come from because they aren't actually in the Bible, is the subject for another book.)

So, while *What about Hitler?* might be a bit of a logic game, it does have significant stakes for what we say and believe about God. It's not hard to say that Hitler was evil. Besides white nationalists and other extremists, who find something about Hitler appealing, everyone else finds the guy's actions and reputation irredeemable. But when we talk about theodicy, about how God works in the world, we must ask whether *anyone* is irredeemable.

Consider people who are in prison or even on death row. Prisons (whether we admit it or not) are based on a model of punishment and not restoration. People who believe in prison abolition as well as those who want to abolish the death penalty often make arguments that highlight the inherent worth of all people, no matter what they've done. That nothing can separate us from the love of God. None of us are irredeemable.

This is a great idea and, without any specific context, is an easy thing to say! But the Hitler question is one that pushes it past all boundaries that allow us to remain in a comfortable spot.

Shouldn't great evil be punished? If God isn't going to punish somebody like Hitler, who will God punish? And what does that say to the survivors and to the people who lost their lives at the hands of this monster? Shouldn't there be some *accountability*? Shouldn't he suffer?

How we answer this question can frame everything else we believe about God. And each person's answer is going to be different from the next person's. It comes with the potential for a complete deconstruction and reconstruction of one's faith. But it also, potentially, helps uncover God's role—active or not—in the problem of evil.

• • •

War

The hits keep coming, right? To think about war theologically we must start with something called *just war theory*.

Just war theory is primarily a form of military ethics, but theologians have long been interested in how we think about the need for military action. Just war theory asks whether a war or military action is *morally justifiable*. Now, there is debate as to whether war—violence—is ever morally justifiable, but let's put that aside momentarily. To make war "moral" it must meet a few criteria that are split into two concepts—the right to go to war and right conduct in war. The first concept helps decide whether the war is morally appropriate and the second is concerned with whether the conduct *during* the war is morally acceptable.

Just war theory acknowledges that war is terrible. But it also believes that some situations (see: Hitler and World War

II) require a response. Or that war is not always the worst option, especially when it comes to preventing genocide.

Opponents of just war theory would argue that violence is never acceptable, especially when it is tied up in politics or nationalist ideology (for example, a country going to war to secure cheap oil prices). And then there are some philosophers and theologians who believe that while war is never morally appropriate, violence can be redemptive—especially when it comes as a part of overthrowing oppressive rulers.

This goes into a previous conversation about God's wrath or, as James Cone describes it, the reality that God is not *for* everybody. God is not a God that supports all sides. Some things are wrong! Some things are evil!

The question becomes: How do we deal with evil? And is violence an appropriate response?

On the one hand, a violent response to an oppressive government would result, one could argue, in a greater good for people who are being hurt.

On the other hand, who gets to decide when violence should be used? And the question of whether violence and war can ever be morally appropriate is not an easy question to answer.

Think about the crucifixion of Jesus for a second. Crucifixion is a form of capital punishment—the death penalty—where the victim is either tied or nailed to a large wooden beam and left to hang until they die from either exhaustion or suffocation. It was and is a vile way to torture a person. It was public. It was meant to dissuade other people from engaging in the same activities as the person being murdered.

Through the cross, God redeems a violent execution—defeats death and a worldly form of torture that is meant to use fear to keep people in line. For many theologians, the cross is an example of the power of redemption—not violence. And so, the thought of *any* violence as being a path toward the Kingdom of God is rejected immediately.

But if God can use the violence of the crucifixion . . . does that mean God can also use the violence of war? And what about World War II? Would it have been morally okay not to intervene? And what about more localized violence, such as police violence against BIPOC (Black, Indigenous, and People of Color) persons in our communities? Does a just war theory trickle down, so to speak, in a way that allows us to normalize violence against people based on the color of their skin or their gender or their sexual identity?

Essentially, you must be comfortable with either justified violence or ignored evil. And then you have to ask—which one better speaks to my concept of God?

• • •

Hunger

There are roughly 7.9 billion people in the world and, according to the United Nations, approximately 700 million people struggle with either food insecurity or not having access to food daily.

This is a tragedy, plain and simple.

There are many reasons for this: Droughts (brought on by climate change?—see below), a growing population, lack of money or job opportunities, the use of food to create products such as biofuel, a lack of sustainable farming skills and practices, and general poverty and sickness in many developing countries.

Of course, if one were so inclined, God could be blamed.

And, well, the same argument kind of applies, right? Why isn't there rain everywhere? Why do we have sickness? Couldn't God create some worldwide extension course for farming skills and practices?

Okay, that last one is kind of a joke.

But this is one of the few topics where blaming God feels more like an out than an honest question.

Because let's face it, there's enough to go around.

And even though there is stuff that is limited—water, food, oil, and fuel sources—that isn't *really* a God thing.

If only we could figure out who caused all this destruction and wasted all these resources . . .

Is it unrealistic to expect an endless supply of the resources we need (want?) to live comfortably? Maybe not. But it is more realistic to take a serious look at how we have been stewards of the resources of the earth. Let's get pointed for a moment. In a global world full of desperate needs, how do we explain when certain countries—ahem, not naming any names here, ahem—choose to center their *wants* over the actual *needs* of developing countries?

Greed, friends.

That's the word we're looking for here.

And it's not just the greed of individuals, because that certainly is a cause of concern. But when we talk about *hunger* or even *poverty*, we are talking about a much greater source of greed—a much greater source of sin in the world.

We live in a world that prizes competition, that tells people they are to blame if they have fallen on hard times and need assistance. And at the same time, it creates an even more insidious narrative that ultimately gets internalized by people who need the most help. Namely, asking for help is a failure. If you can't pull yourself up by your own bootstraps, you're a failure. Just work a little harder.

This is a critique of capitalism, which might be hard to hear if it's your first time. But capitalism, the idea of a "free market," is fundamentally at odds not only with the idea that everybody deserves a chance to be happy and healthy but, some would suggest, with God! In the Bible, there are more than eight hundred mentions of money, including the idea of *jubilee*, which was an opportunity to "reset" the financial and material state of the Jewish community—a chance to fix inequalities, to make sure that nobody was born into generational poverty and suffering.

How we use our resources matters.

And, to be frank, this is not a question of theodicy as much as it is a question of God pleading with us to take care of one another.

• • •

Cancer

This one requires a light touch.

More than likely, you know somebody who has been affected by cancer, and if you don't, you likely will at some point in your life.

Cancer is hard. Cancer is awful for everyone involved. Cancer is the epitome of suffering.

Feel free to skip this one, okay?

How do we think about cancer in light of a theological conversation about God and the problem of evil? In some ways, there's nothing new here—it hits all the same points we've been circling for much of our time together. Did God create cancer? Why does God let cancer exist?

Et cetera, et cetera, et cetera.

This doesn't mean that these questions are any less important. In some ways, a conversation about cancer—about terminal illnesses of all kinds—might be *the most important* one we can have from a theological lens, especially since these questions are so prevalent and, for many people, are the first time they are angry with God. The first time they demand and answer to the big question of *why?*

Again, care for yourself here.

But the answer, if there is one, might be about the result of so many choices that prioritize greed or take advantage of the environment, all of it causing conditions that either helped to create cancer *or* did not allow the conditions for a cure—something—to be developed outside of the capitalist, insurance, and medical structures that prioritize profit.

This does not mean that doctors, nurses, or any other health care workers are responsible for cancer! They, too, suffer under the same system of predatory neglect as the rest of us.

So where is God in all of this?

Can we blame God for not overriding the system, so to speak, and just curing cancer?

And let's talk about miracles for a second—who gets them? Why are some cancers miraculously cured? Why are some cancers terminal, leaving the patient with only months or weeks to live?

The answer to that question often leaves people with a feeling of doubt and emptiness. Why would God prioritize one person's life and not another's? The answer is quite simple: God does *not* prioritize one person's life over another's.

One way people answer this is asking, "What does it mean to heal? Can healing look like acceptance, like dying well?"

Yes. Of course. And for many people, the idea of *quality* of life at the end of their life becomes more important that *quantity*. There's no right answer here. For some people, fighting like hell is the answer. For others, it means spending as much time with their family as they can.

Healing looks different for different people.

Unfortunately, there isn't much one can say about cancer that isn't either deeply unsatisfying or totally inappropriate. While this is a great time to acknowledge the importance of a thoughtful theodicy in moments such as this, it's also important to remember that *good theology* is good until it isn't.

Meaning: Sometimes there is no answer, no justification.

Sometimes you just have to sit with a friend or a family member and be angry. To cry. To take it one day at a time.

●　●　●

An Addendum to Discuss COVID-19

We've been through our first global pandemic and whether you believe COVID is real (it is) or you believe that same uncle who lives up in Alaska in a bunker wearing a tinfoil hat (speaks for itself), the question of *why* has been prevalent for many people during the past couple of years.

There isn't much new information outside of what we've already discussed above. One way to think about COVID is that it is a *natural evil*—like tornadoes or hurricanes.

It's tempting to put COVID into that category.

However, the question of responsibility quickly becomes relevant.

Not in terms of who created COVID or why pandemics occur.

Instead, we face the question of personal responsibility and the desire to lift individual "rights" (which are almost always closer to "preferences") over the well-being of the rest of the world. Of politicians and pundits who decide to politicize the pandemic, to make vaccines a debatable topic.

Again, this one feels less about God and more about a population of intensely selfish people who would rather make other people sick than inconvenience their lives in even the smallest of ways.

• • •

Climate Change

When we talk about climate change, which also includes the extinction of species, we must start at the story of creation. No matter how you think about creation and the creation stories, it is important to think about the difference between truth and Truth.

Oh, this is about to get good. This is something you can *really* use.

When we think of a biblical story, there are layers of truth involved. We can read the creation narrative as True (meaning: there is a greater, perhaps universal lesson to be learned from this story) while also acknowledging that it might not be factually *true*.

Get that? Upper case Truth is universal. Lower case truth is often factual.

They don't have to go together. Sometimes a story will be both. And sometimes we must suspend our rational minds to look for the Truth of a story.

Like, was Jonah swallowed by a whale?

Seems kind of fishy. (You're welcome. I'm sorry.)

But even if it *isn't* true, isn't there something important about knowing that God will call us to places we don't expect—to welcome in people we might not think are a part of the group?

So, Truth. And truth.

Okay, back to creation.

It feels *slightly* inappropriate—if not completely comical—to suggest that, somehow, God didn't make the world in a way that would allow it to be self-sustaining. To be, to use a different word, *eternal.* And before somebody brings it up, no this is not a place where you can argue that God is creating a new earth—that earth is somehow a temporary stop for all of us, so it doesn't matter what we do to it here and now. The idea of "new earth" is a theological construct that helps us remember—and look for—the work that God is doing in the world. It's a hope in the future, even when we can't see a way forward.

But it doesn't mean we should all drive gas-guzzling SUVs.

Now, it's true that the Bible was constructed and written during a time when there was no industry—at least not in the way we have now. So, pollution, global warming, the very real chance that the world might eventually be uninhabitable, was not necessarily a concern.

And yet, woven through these stories is a message of *stewardship*. A responsibility—you could call it a moral responsibility—to steward the resources of the planet in a way that makes the world sustainable for your kids, your grandkids—for generation after generation.

Hey, it's starting to seem like, for a lot of these issues, it's more of an *us* problem than a *God* problem.

Weird, right?

This is where process theology, once again, might have an insight for us. Process theology believes that God and the earth are inseparable, so what we do to the earth is literally doing the same thing to God. It also warns that believing in the traditional *omnis* might create a sense of complacency that ultimately ends with the world . . . ending.

Because if the world ends, that means God wants the world to end!

If this sounds troublesome or incorrect . . . you're not alone.

Of course, some people will call climate change a *natural evil*, akin to floods and hurricanes and . . . *stop. Please stop.*

We are responsible. We are obligated.

And it is not out of bounds to say that God cares about the health of the planet.

It makes things pretty simple, doesn't it?

• • •

A Quick Word on Prayer

You can't really discuss theodicy without talking about prayer, even briefly. Even people who are not religious often find themselves in moments of distress calling out to something greater than themselves. This is the idea that there are "no atheists in foxholes," that during something as traumatic as war even the staunchest nonbeliever might look for divine intervention.

For people of faith, prayer is a natural part of our life. It's a spiritual practice, something we do to cultivate a relationship with God. However, prayer is not without its controversies, for lack of a better word.

People pray for victories in football games.

People pray for healing.

People ask God to smite their enemies.

People ask not to be smote by God.

Some of these prayers *work* and some of them feel like God is not only not listening but doesn't even have the decency to let you know that the message has been read.

So, does prayer work?

Yes. But perhaps not often in the ways we think it should or could. Much like theodicy, the answer here often feels like a dodge, a way to explain God's absence. But prayer is about the relationship, about the constant conversation—the invitation to be intentionally in God's presence on a regular basis throughout our lives.

We don't have to believe in a God who intervenes in the world to believe that prayer is nourishing and good.

There are definitely prayers that are meant to change circumstances, and that's not the only reason for this spiritual practice. Sometimes we pray to get through difficult times, to remember that God is always present and near us. Sometimes we pray to thank God, or to *glorify* God, which is meant to be a comfort—an acknowledgment that God is eternal. And we pray when we come together as a community of faith each week, asking God to be active in the world and in our lives, to help us look for ways to reconcile—to find peace and wholeness.

Does this help?

Maybe.

Does it hurt?

Probably not.

● ● ●

Okay, that was . . . a lot.

Like, a *whole* lot.

You might be thinking: well, this wasn't very helpful, which is starting to seem par for the course, right? Often, the work of theology is not to give us an answer but to clear away some of the scrub brush that litters the trail we're trying to walk. The work of clearing helps us get rid of some of the obvious *wrong* answers—the ones we intrinsically know will cause harm either to ourselves or to others.

To put it a different way, we're figuring out what we *can* and *cannot* say about God. This, in fancy theological terms, is called *apophatic theology* and *cataphatic theology*.

We can say that God loves us (*cataphatic*).

We cannot say that God has left us alone (*apophatic*).

And this leads us to a question that may have a very clear answer for you or . . . might not.

Is the world getting better or worse?

How we answer this can give us another clue about how we think about God's action or inaction in the world. One answer is to think about how our actions and inactions, the inability for humans to compassionately acknowledge and address evil, cause pain and suffering in the world. Rabbi Harold Kushner, in his book *When Bad Things Happen to Good People,* would say that God does God's best but is unable to fully prevent suffering. Or, even more powerful, that *our* actions in the face of suffering is *God at work in us*.

This might not solve the problem of *why*, but it does force us to ask the question: What can I do?

11

Right, but I Want an Actual, Concrete Answer

It's wonderfully ironic that—outside of the Necessary Interludes—this will likely be one of the shortest chapters in this book.

The answer chapter!

Let's see if we can get to five pages!

Listen, we warned you. We told you that answers were going to be few and far between in this book. So, what we're trying to say is that you can only blame yourself.

Kidding. (Kind of.)

But if there is a moral to this conversation, perhaps it's found in the power of saying *I don't know*. Or to put it a different way, finding the theological power in being able to accept some mystery in our relationship with God.

Does this seem like yet another dodge?

Oh, it's most certainly a dodge.

When you're faced with Big Questions, the ones that affect our lives in meaningful and challenging ways, the search for an answer can become, quite literally, destructive.

And listen, it's not like we don't have *evidence* of goodness as a part of our life of faith. One of the most important aspects of the church is not the theology or doctrine (of course, that does matter!), it's the community. If you're a part of a church community, you likely know this already, even if you can't articulate it.

There's that one person you see only at church.

There's that one person who always checks up on you.

And maybe there's that surrogate grandmother, who always has weird but tasty hard candies that she slips you right after you've received the Eucharist.

> Holy Eucharist, or Holy Communion, or simply the Eucharist (which means "thanksgiving") is one of the sacraments (a ritual that transmits God's grace) of the church. Think of it like a family meal and a taste of the heavenly banquet we'll share with God. From there, opinions and theologies vary *widely*—but know that God invites all of us, no matter what, to participate and receive this meal.

This community, these relationships, are evidence of the goodness of God. And while they might not be a practical answer to the question of evil or why bad things happen, they are a starting point.

If we can come together in this found family of Church and worship together—if we can confess our sins, be absolved, all while celebrating the joys of life right alongside the painful moments, that *means something*. It happens when we welcome a new child of God to the church through baptism, when we approach the altar to experience the mystery of receiving communion together, when we gather to send people out into the world to follow a calling, when we celebrate the resurrection of life and the defeat of death during funerals.

> Baptism is another sacrament of the church, one where people at any age, depending on the denomination, are adopted into God's family—the Church—and reminded that nothing can separate us from the love of God. It can happen by pouring water or total immersion (dunking!) and it marks a public renunciation of evil—saying, "I'm ready, God."

These are all answers to the problem of evil.

All of these proclaim to the world that we do not have to live in suffering.

We do not have to bow down to evil.

This is an answer. Likely not the answer you were looking to find. But it's an answer, even in a small way.

And perhaps this is simply the place we start.

A good theology doesn't mean a theology that solves every single problem. Nothing will ever be completely buttoned up on this side of Jordan, as the country preachers might say. Theology is inherently messy. A beautiful kind of messy, yes—but pretty darn messy all the same! It is almost never black and white. It can be frustrating and chaotic and, when you least expect it, shockingly relevant to your life in ways you may never comprehend.

When we think theologically, we accept a bit of a bargain with God. We are given the gift of discernment, a way to test the adequacy of answers that are offered to us (*everybody* has opinions about this stuff). And the more we test these questions, these answers, the more we start to figure out what we believe.

The more we start to see God a little more clearly.

Ultimately, that's what this is all about—being rooted in God. Knowing, as the prophet Isaiah says, that we are called and known by name.

12

An Entirely Too Short (Like, Really, What Are We Thinking?) Chapter on Heaven and Hell

A lot of people use the existence of heaven and hell as the ultimate theological *get out of jail free* card. An afterlife provides a sense of finality—a way to not only help us sleep easier at night but to absolve God from the problem of evil.

Heaven and hell make sense, right?

You live your life the right way and—Ding! Ding!— the elevator to heaven shows up and away you go, flying toward eternity with all your friends and family, your dog, living in that 20-bedroom mansion, spending eternity doing whatever you like because, *heaven.*

It's a reward, justification for all the crap you put up with—the crap you survived on earth.

Frankly, it's the least God could do.

Hell, naturally, works similarly. Live your life the wrong way and—watch out!—that trap door is going to open and from there it's nothing but an eternal slide into the fire, facing deserved punishment and, hey, you might also see some friends down there—*who knows!*

All joking aside, our theology about heaven and hell matters—whether you believe in them or not—because it requires us to think through questions about accountability, punishment, divine justice, and how God balances the proverbial score sheet when it comes to sins big and small.

But what sins are big enough to send us to hell? And is it a cumulative effect or are there certain things that, if we do them, are just *so bad* there is no saving us from the consequences? And why does hell even exist? Doesn't it run counter to, like, everything we believe about God's eternal love?

Before we go much further, let's be clear: you don't have to believe in an afterlife. You don't have to believe in heaven or hell and, frankly, a lot of what people *do* believe isn't in the Bible, so just know that none of this is as black and white as people want you to think.

Okay, let's start with heaven.

In the Christian tradition, heaven is a place that ranges from the proverbial streets of gold to a never-ending worship experience where we spend eternity praising and glorifying God. For some, it's a family reunion—a chance to corner Socrates or maybe Elvis and pick their brain for, well, as long as you want because you literally have eternity. And then there's the halos, the harps, the wings—oh, wait, those are for angels, *not us*. Not even after we die. And that doesn't even get into the books, television shows, movies, plays, the truly terrible and trauma-inducing art, and epic poems—all of which introduce *new* concepts about heaven—and let's just say that people have spent *a lot* of time trying to figure out what heaven might be like and, of course, what we need to do to get there.

Let's talk about angels for a second. First, it isn't the classic white robes and little, um, angelic faces. You've got *Seraphim* (literally translated as "burning ones") who are at the top of the angelic class. Imagine this: six wings, human hands, voices, and constantly singing God's praises, *Holy, holy, holy is the Lord Almighty; the whole earth is full of God's glory.* Next, *Cherubim,* who aren't freaky at all with their four faces—a man, an ox, a lion, and an eagle—and four wings covered in eyes. Oh, yeah, they also have a lion's body and the feet of an ox. These are the ones who guarded the Garden of Eden—fiery swords, all that. From there, angels are separated into various hierarchies that include Thrones, Virtues, Archangels, and plain old angels, which are the ones that usually are sent as messengers to humans. Long story short, if you encounter an angel, your life is likely to get *really* complicated.

But what do we *actually know* about heaven?

In traditional Christianity, heaven is the "dwelling place" of God and the angels—the location of God's (actual?)

throne. For some Christians, heaven is temporary—a place where we wait until the resurrection of the dead and the return of all the saints to the New Earth that God has created in the world. In fact, early Christians didn't really think about heaven much, as they were convinced that Jesus was coming back in their lifetime. There was an urgency to their faith, a sense that everything was happening *right then* and they needed to be a part of this new thing that was occurring in (and to) the world. When Jesus didn't come back, Christian theology slowly changed to include the idea of heaven as a place we go to after we die.

However, what if we could reclaim some of that urgency now? What if we could connect it to the idea of a God who has defeated death—who not only cares for us eternally, but is intimately present *right now*?

What might that world look like?

> *New Earth* is an expression used to describe the final state of a redeemed—saved, if you like that sort of language—world. It's fundamentally important to the idea of Christian salvation and can be found in Isaiah 65:17, 65:22; 2 Peter 3:13, and most notably Revelation 21:1. It's also referenced in the Nicene Creed—*the world to come*. The best way to think about it: it's the final product of the ongoing work of God in the world.

Hell, as you might guess, has gotten much of the same treatment. In fact, maybe more because, let's face it, it's a little more exciting—fun?—to imagine hell.

On its most basic level, hell, in Christian theology, is often the device used to explain where and how God's judgment is executed.

> In the Bible, the word that is commonly translated as "hell" means different things.
>
> **Sheol**, found in the Hebrew Bible, is a temporary place where the dead stay—an underworld, of sorts, similar to the Greek idea of Hades. Which is interesting, since it's translated as both "grave" and, at certain points in the New Testament . . . "Hades."
>
> **Gehenna**, in the New Testament, is what most people imagine when they think of hell. It's the "unquenchable fire" (Matthew 10:28) that can destroy both body and soul. (This is where the term *hellfire* comes from, too.) However, Gehenna wasn't a spiritual place—it was a physical location, outside the city of Jerusalem, where people burned garbage and outcasts, such as lepers, were sent.

Most of the theology around hell is inferred from various Bible passages, pagan myths, and medieval poets.

Theologians (it's always the theologians, am I right? *Paging Mr. Augustine!*) essentially painted themselves into a corner when it comes to the idea of hell. If we have free will and reject a relationship with God—and if we know that God will not force this relationship—then there *must* be some sort of consequence for this act of rebellion. If not, then how can God's justice and mercy be true?

Do you smell that?

It smells fishy—straight out of the ocean, still on the hook, *fishy.*

Let's consider some of what the Bible says—specifically the parables of Jesus, which might seem concerning. Especially if read literally. (And, hey, the very fact that they're *parables* means they're not supposed to be read literally!)

In one such passage—Matthew 25:31–46—Jesus tells a story about a king who separates people into two categories—sheep and goats. The sheep (those who gave hungry people food, welcomed strangers, clothed the naked, took care of the sick, and visited prisoners) will all "inherit the kingdom." Whereas the goats—the ones who did *not* do these things—will be left for the eternal fire.

Harsh, right?

In another passage, this time in the Gospel of Luke (16:19–31) we hear a story—again, a parable—of a rich man and a poor man. The poor man ends up in heaven and the rich man, who saw the suffering of the poor man and did nothing while they were both on earth, ends up in "Hades" and sees Abraham (from the Old Testament) hanging out with Lazarus, the poor man, and says, "Father Abraham, have mercy on me, and send Lazarus to dip the tip of his finger in water and cool my tongue; for I am in agony in these flames" (Luke 16:24).

Again, harsh.

But what do we *learn* from these stories?

Some people would definitely say, "A clear picture of *heaven* and *hell*."

Is that the message you think we're supposed to get from these stories? Does that literal reading limit our imagination, the dream of what God *can* do?

Of what we should do?

Both parables stress the importance of taking care of other people—especially those in need, whom Jesus calls the "least of these." (And it's interesting to note in the second parable that there's no mention of anything Lazarus has done that earns him a place in "the bosom of Abraham." What could that mean?) We're given a glimpse of God's vision for the world. If we're willing to see it—willing to suspend our human-derived ideas about theology and how God *should* work in the world.

What if we read these parables—the entire story of God—not as an *us* and *them* story but instead as simply an *us* story? What if the point of these parables is not to show us who is in and who is out, but a reminder that we are made to be co-creators—collaborators—in the work of building and bringing forth the kingdom of heaven—the dwelling-place of God?

> The Kingdom of God is a phrase from the Bible, meant to help us see and understand the work of God in the world—a future (and ongoing) reality that is rebuilding the world to look the way it should. Right here. Not in some distant heavenly future. Over time, some have had trouble with the male-oriented and imperialistic word *kingdom*. To acknowledge that, people will often use *reign* or even *kin-dom* which is a substitute offered by feminist theologians.

This is about how we're supposed to live, not what happens when we die. Through this work, we live into the vision God has for us and for the world. A vision that is a restoration of Eden, a world of peace and justice and mercy, because that's what God has always intended for all of us.

Through these parables—and our own work in the world—we are reminded of *our* creation story, the one that tells us we've been created in God's image. It's a chance to see the *imago Dei* not only in ourselves—but in our friends, our neighbors, and yeah, even our enemies.

To read the Bible—to live our lives—like this is a recipe for being surprised—the *good* kind of shocked.

And it puts us in good company.

Take a second and read the parables found in Luke 15.

This is a God who *relentlessly* searches us out—a lost coin, a stray sheep, a prodigal child—reminding us that we're never so lost or so separated that we can't return to God's love and grace. And when we finally come back into the fold, it's to the biggest and best party we've ever seen.

The parables of the Lost Sheep, the Lost Coin, and the Prodigal Son are stories of redemption, a picture of a God who is searching for *you* no matter where you go—no matter what you do. It tells us that reconciliation can happen to anybody at any time. For some, that's dangerous—enough so that they have to build entire theologies to refute it.

For others, it's called the Good News.

So what do *you* want to believe about God?

Do you want to believe in a God who is keeping track of every mistake we make, adding another pebble to the divine scale of judgment? Or do you want to believe in a God who understands that we make mistakes and still searches us out?

If you're not completely sold yet, ask yourself: Who do you say God is?

More than likely it's going to involve *love*.

And no matter what some nerdy systematic theologian in a basement seminary office might have to say about the matter, let's remember once again that saying that God loves us is about as profound a theological statement that we can make. A revolutionary statement. The sort of statement that subverts everything the world says is important.

So, let's ask the big question—maybe the only one that really matters—when you talk about heaven and hell.

Would a God who loves you *unconditionally* ever send you to hell?

No.

Hear it again: *No.*

There are some traditional Christians who are right now crossing themselves and saying a prayer because this flies in the face of how Christianity has often understood eschatology, or the act of God's salvation. Often called *universal salvation* or *universal reconciliation*, it basically means that God is going to redeem (or save) the world—no matter what.

Does this bring up more problems?

Oh yeah.

Will it get people huffing and puffing?

If you listen closely, you can already hear them.

13

God Is Good (or, the End of This Book, Which Is Actually the Beginning)

Okay, here's the last bad (Dad?) joke of the book. And it's a *Bible* joke! So you know it's going to be good—inspired, even. (That one is free.)

The last shall be first.

That's a joke. A pretty good one, too. Theological, even! Which are, of course, the best kinds of jokes, right? And listen, this one came from *Jesus.*

All joking aside, this is the end of the book—but it's also the beginning.

You've wrestled with some intense questions in this book. And, unless you're not telling us something, you did so without suffering one of those Jacob hip injuries. Well done! It's important to stretch the way you think theologically, not only for yourself but also for your friends and family.

Because at some point, this is going to be relevant.

At some point, you'll come across a question that cannot be answered and, if nothing else has been evident during our time together, it's this: there are precious few solid answers.

Let's once again remind ourselves that this is actually good news.

No, really.

The work we have before us is recognizing and naming the Reign/Kingdom/Kin-dom of God in the world. It's helping other people see the suffering, being aware that the world needs some help—that we all need some help. We are called to be co-conspirators in the wild and subversive work of proclaiming hope and sowing seeds of compassion, of looking for cracks of light in the darkness.

The answer is the work.

This is both a blessing and a curse! You no longer have the privilege of justifying the evil you come across. You can no longer encounter suffering and explain it away as normal.

So, accept this benediction—this sending forth.

Find compassion in the world.

Believe in the power of love and the transfer of power to those who do not have it.

Above all, remember that the world is moving toward redemption and reconciliation. Toward a future where liberation and love rule.

Amen?

Amen!

14

A Totally Optional Postlude

You did it.

The end of the road. The last chapter. The *it looks like God really does answer prayers* moment when you can close this book and never think about theodicy ever again. Well, probably not . . . but let's not get too worked up about that because . . .

You're *done*!

Let's check in one last time.

How are you doing?

What's got your mind working—your soul stirring?

Are you feeling fulfilled or are you wishing there was just *a little bit more*?

If you could ask one question, what would it be?

No matter how you're feeling, congratulate yourself on accomplishing something important. There are so many people who sweep their big questions under the rug. You didn't do that. You took every shot theodicy had to give and you're still standing—that's a big deal.

No, seriously.

Theology can be faked, wrapped up in fancy language that ultimately means nothing when the proverbial crap hits the fan. Real theology is hard. It requires investment. It asks you to care, to risk discomfort, and to believe that God is, even in the smallest way, knowable.

That's good, hard stuff.

You deserve a round of applause.

Or a snack (maybe it's time for that ice cream).

Or even a nap.

Hey, after all this—you decide.